JavaScript for PHP Developers

Stoyan Stefanov

O'REILLY®

Beijing · Cambridge · Farnham · Köln · Sebastopol · Tokyo

JavaScript for PHP Developers

by Stoyan Stefanov

Printed in the United States of America.

Published by O'Reilly Media, Inc., 1005 Gravenstein Highway North, Sebastopol, CA 95472.

O'Reilly books may be purchased for educational, business, or sales promotional use. Online editions are also available for most titles (*http://my.safaribooksonline.com*). For more information, contact our corporate/institutional sales department: 800-998-9938 or *corporate@oreilly.com*.

Editor: Mary Treseler	**Indexer:** Meghan Jones, WordCo Indexing
Production Editor: Kara Ebrahim	**Cover Designer:** Randy Comer
Copyeditor: Amanda Kersey	**Interior Designer:** David Futato
Proofreader: Jasmine Kwityn	**Illustrator:** Rebecca Demarest

April 2013:   First Edition

Revision History for the First Edition:

2013-04-24:   First release

See *http://oreilly.com/catalog/errata.csp?isbn=9781449320195* for release details.

ISBN: 978-1-449-32019-5

[LSI]

To Nathalie, Zlatina, and Eva

Table of Contents

Acknowledgments

First and foremost, big thanks and gratitude to my second-time reviewers who helped me with *JavaScript Patterns* before, the Three Musketeers and d'Artagnan: the ever-so-amazing Andrea Giammarchi, Asen Bozhilov, Dmitry Soshnikov, and Juriy "kangax" Zaytsev. As with the previous book, they helped me tremendously with their deep knowledge and experience with JavaScript, their attention to detail, and their determination to have technical accuracy above all. They would often comment on some of my bold general statements with: "Hmm, this is not entirely correct and not always true, because...." I am forever in debt to these four ridiculously talented developers who also happen to be great and friendly people.

Many thanks to Chris Shiflett and Sean Coates. They made sure the PHP side of things made sense, but what's more, this whole book started as a post on their PHPAdvent (now WebAdvent.org) blog, followed by a talk at the ConFoo conference, which Sean helps organize.

Next, thanks to the Facebook engineers who hang out in the JavaScript group. I posted an early draft there asking for comments. Three people even went through the whole thing and gave me invaluable feedback and further nitpicking, which is the best quality in a technical reviewer. Thanks to Alok Menghrajani, James Ide, and Alex Himel.

Finally, thanks to Randy Owens who read the "early release" of the book and meticulously filed tens of errata reports.

—Stoyan Stefanov
Los Angeles, April 2013

Preface

JavaScript is the language of the browser. It's also the language that allows you to build increasingly diverse types of client, server, desktop, mobile, and shell applications. HTML5 continues the trend of allowing you to build rich applications (formerly known as RIA, Ajax, and DHTML) with new features such as local storage, databases on the client, geolocation, image, and audio and video APIs—all exposed and scriptable with JavaScript. Fluency in JavaScript is a must for every web developer today.

This book is for the PHP developer who's learning JavaScript from the ground up. Both languages look deceptively close because they both share the similar C-like syntax. But they differ in many concepts, such as object creation, classes, and prototypes, which are critical to mastering each language. The book draws on your previous experience and so it won't put you to sleep explaining the most trivial topics such as conditions and loops. At the same time, the book is a complete reference: all the important information is here, emphasizing the differences with PHP and glossing over the similarities.

Conventions Used in This Book

The following typographical conventions are used in this book:

Italic
> Indicates new terms, URLs, email addresses, filenames, and file extensions.

`Constant width`
> Used for program listings, as well as within paragraphs to refer to program elements such as variable or function names, databases, data types, environment variables, statements, and keywords.

`Constant width bold`
> Shows commands or other text that should be typed literally by the user.

Constant width italic

> Shows text that should be replaced with user-supplied values or by values determined by context.

  This icon signifies a tip, suggestion, or general note.

  This icon indicates a warning or caution.

Using Code Examples

This book is here to help you get your job done. In general, if this book includes code examples, you may use the code in this book in your programs and documentation. You do not need to contact us for permission unless you're reproducing a significant portion of the code. For example, writing a program that uses several chunks of code from this book does not require permission. Selling or distributing a CD-ROM of examples from O'Reilly books does require permission. Answering a question by citing this book and quoting example code does not require permission. Incorporating a significant amount of example code from this book into your product's documentation does require permission.

We appreciate, but do not require, attribution. An attribution usually includes the title, author, publisher, and ISBN. For example: "*JavaScript for PHP Developers* by Stoyan Stefanov (O'Reilly). Copyright 2013 Stoyan Stefanov, 978-1-449-32019-5."

If you feel your use of code examples falls outside fair use or the permission given above, feel free to contact us at *permissions@oreilly.com*.

Safari® Books Online

Safari. *Safari Books Online* is an on-demand digital library that delivers expert content in both book and video form from the world's leading authors in technology and business.

Technology professionals, software developers, web designers, and business and creative professionals use Safari Books Online as their primary resource for research, problem solving, learning, and certification training.

Safari Books Online offers a range of product mixes and pricing programs for organizations, government agencies, and individuals. Subscribers have access to thousands of books, training videos, and prepublication manuscripts in one fully searchable database from publishers like O'Reilly Media, Prentice Hall Professional, Addison-Wesley Professional, Microsoft Press, Sams, Que, Peachpit Press, Focal Press, Cisco Press, John Wiley & Sons, Syngress, Morgan Kaufmann, IBM Redbooks, Packt, Adobe Press, FT Press, Apress, Manning, New Riders, McGraw-Hill, Jones & Bartlett, Course Technology, and dozens more. For more information about Safari Books Online, please visit us online.

How to Contact Us

Please address comments and questions concerning this book to the publisher:

O'Reilly Media, Inc.
1005 Gravenstein Highway North
Sebastopol, CA 95472
800-998-9938 (in the United States or Canada)
707-829-0515 (international or local)
707-829-0104 (fax)

We have a web page for this book, where we list errata, examples, and any additional information. You can access this page at *http://oreil.ly/javascript-php*.

To comment or ask technical questions about this book, send email to *bookques tions@oreilly.com*.

For more information about our books, courses, conferences, and news, see our website at *http://www.oreilly.com*.

Find us on Facebook: *http://facebook.com/oreilly*

Follow us on Twitter: *http://twitter.com/oreillymedia*

Watch us on YouTube: *http://www.youtube.com/oreillymedia*

CHAPTER 1

Introduction

JavaScript has had a bad reputation for years. Many developers consider writing in JavaScript a pain because the programs behave so unpredictably. Once done coding, they open another browser to test, only to be greeted with an unhelpful error message (Figure 1-1). Thus, developers often simply refuse to bother studying the language.

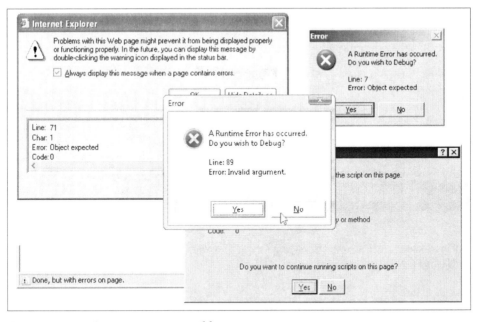

Figure 1-1. JavaScript errors gone wild

As it turns out, most of the problems have historically been (and let's be honest, still are) due to browser differences in the implementation of DOM and BOM, and to a much smaller extent, the JavaScript language itself.

DOM stands for Document Object Model. It's an API (application programming interface) for working with structured documents such as those written in XML, XHTML, and HTML. DOM is a *language-independent* API that also exists in PHP (*http://php.net/dom*). In JavaScript, this API is easily spotted: anything that starts with `document.` has to do with the DOM. As a point of historical interest, DOM started in JavaScript and was later standardized by the World Wide Web Consortium (W3C) as an API independent of JavaScript or any other language. These days, you can still unearth remnants of that primordial DOM (now called DOM0)—things like `document.images` (all images on a page) and `document.links` (all links), which were replaced in DOM version 1 with more generic methods such as `document.getElementById()` and `document.getEle mentsByTagName()`.

BOM stands for Browser Object Model. It's a nice name for something that's not formally defined. It's a collection of browser-related properties and methods, such as available screen size or the status bar. Most of these properties are available as globals such as `innerWidth`, although you most often see them used as properties of the `window` object (e.g., `window.innerWidth`). BOM hasn't been standardized for a long time, so as you can imagine, there are some differences across browsers. HTML5 started to codify common behavior among browsers, including the common BOM objects.

Another term you need to know is *ECMAScript*. This is the core JavaScript language when you strip out the DOM and BOM. It's the language that deals with syntax, loops, functions, objects, and so on. JavaScript started as a Netscape innovation, but was later copied by other browser vendors, raising the need for this language to establish a standard to which all implementors (browser vendors and others) would need to conform. This standard was defined by the European Computer Manufacturers Association (ECMA), now Ecma International, and called ECMAScript. These days, JavaScript should technically mean Mozilla's implementation of ECMAScript (there's also JScript, which is Microsoft's implementation), but that's not what people mean when they say "JavaScript."

All in all, when people talk about JavaScript, they may mean an array of topics, including DOM, BOM, and ECMAScript. So:

JavaScript = ECMAScript + DOM + BOM

Scope of This Book

A good thing that has happened since the early days of the Web is that now there is a wide availability of high-quality JavaScript libraries, such as jQuery and YUI (Yahoo!

User Interface Library). These libraries take the pain out of development by providing an API layer that abstracts the differences in the browser implementations of DOM and BOM—and sometimes ECMAScript itself.

The scope of this book is ECMAScript, the language itself. DOM is something you're probably already familiar with from PHP, and BOM is not really that interesting (it's just a collection of global variables and functions). Plus, you can always use a library to abstract the DOM and BOM. This book is independent of any particular JavaScript library, allowing you to focus on the core language and pick a library of your choice when you need one.

The book uses the term JavaScript to mean ECMAScript because using "ECMAScript" is uncommon and just plain awkward. The focus is on the most popular version of the language, ECMAScript 3 (ES3). The standards body skipped version 4 and the latest version at the time of this book's publication is ECMAScript 5.1, which is also referred to as ES5. Although ES5 is already widely available, you cannot rely on it if you want to support older browsers, such as Internet Explorer before version 9. Chapter 6 details what's new and different in ES5, and will help you to decide whether or not to use it. It works even in old browsers via a "shim," or "polyfill," as you'll see in "Shims" on page 112.

The Language

Once you strip out all the DOM/BOM browser hell, what you have left is JavaScript—a beautiful, small language with a familiar C-like syntax and just a handful of built-in objects.

It's a popular language that's practically everywhere: on the client, server, mobile phones, desktop, and shell. Even inside PHP you can embed JavaScript using the V8Js PHP class. It's actually harder to find an environment where you *cannot* run JavaScript, which means you can learn one language and use it everywhere.

It's also an odd language when you approach it from the perspective of a PHP developer. Here are some things to be aware of early on and look for as you progress through this book:

- Functions in JavaScript are *objects*. Arrays and regular expressions are objects, too.
- Functions provide *scope*, and local variable scope is achieved by wrapping the code in a function.
- *Closures* are used heavily. Although closures have existed in PHP since version 5.3, they are not yet commonly used in PHP. In JavaScript, they are everywhere.
- *Prototypes* are an important concept in JavaScript for which there is no equivalent in PHP. It's one of the ways JavaScript accomplishes code reuse and inheritance.

- JavaScript doesn't have a concept of *classes*. This is really odd from a PHP perspective and will be discussed in detail.

Learning Environment

((("environment"To keep things simple, you don't need to get bogged down with creating and maintaining a user interface. JavaScript doesn't have a concept of input and output. I/O is provided by the environment that JavaScript programs run in. The most common environment is the web browser, where the responsibility for a user interface falls to HTML. You don't need all that to study the language, so let's just use the I/O provided by a JavaScript console.

A console lets you quickly type pieces of code and see them run, just like the interactive PHP shell you invoke on the command line:

```
$ php -a
Interactive shell

php > echo "hi";
hi
```

There are many JavaScript consoles to pick from and use for studying. The most accessible consoles are those provided by browsers.

Browsers

In a desktop WebKit browser (e.g., Chrome or Safari), simply load a page, right-click anywhere, and select "Inspect element" from the menu. This brings up the Web Inspector. Click the Console tab and you're ready to go (Figure 1-2).

In newer Firefox versions, you get to a console by going to the Menu Bar and selecting Tools→Web Developer→Web Console. Alternatively, you can also install the Firebug extension, which works in any Firefox version.

Internet Explorer (since IE8) has F12 Developer Tools with a console under the Script tab.

Figure 1-2. Web Inspector console

JavaScriptCore

If you're on a Mac, it already comes with a JavaScript interpreter capable of running shell scripts. Windows has a built-in command-line JavaScript interpreter, too, but lacks a console.

The JavaScript command-line interpreter on a Mac is a program called JavaScriptCore, which can be found in */System/Library/Frameworks/JavaScriptCore.framework/ Versions/Current/Resources/jsc.*

You can make an alias to it so that it's easier to find:

1. Launch the Terminal application (e.g., by typing "terminal" in Spotlight).
2. Type the following:

   ```
   alias jsc='/System/Library/Frameworks/JavaScriptCore.framework/Versions/
              Current/Resources/jsc'
   ```
3. Now you can launch the console by typing `jsc` (Figure 1-3).

```
● ○ ○                    ⌂ stoyanstefanov — jsc — 80×24
stoyanstefmbp15:~ stoyanstefanov$ alias jsc='/System/Library/Frameworks/JavaScri
ptCore.framework/Versions/Current/Resources/jsc'
stoyanstefmbp15:~ stoyanstefanov$ jsc
> 1 + 1
2
> var a = 1; var b = 2 + a;
undefined
> b;
3
> ▋
```

Figure 1-3. JavaScriptCore console

Note that this is an even more pristine environment than the browser's console because it has no concept of BOM and DOM, just the core JavaScript language.

Feel free to add the `alias` line to your `~/.profile` so that it's always there when you need it.

 The JavaScriptCore engine is used in WebKit-based browsers, but not in Chrome, which has its own JavaScript engine called V8.

Node.js and Rhino

If you install Node.js or Rhino on your computer, you can use their consoles, which have the benefit of working on any operating system.

Node.js (*http://nodejs.org*) is based on Google's V8 JavaScript engine. After you install it, you can type **node** in the Terminal to get the console (Figure 1-4).

```
● ○ ○                    ⌂ stoyanstefanov — node — 80×24
stoyanstefmbp15:~ stoyanstefanov$ node
> var h = "hello";
undefined
> h;
'hello'
> h + " node console!";
'hello node console!'
> ▋
```

Figure 1-4. Node.js console

Rhino (*http://www.mozilla.org/rhino/*) is a JavaScript interpreter by Mozilla written in Java. After you download the *rhino.jar* file and save it where you find appropriate (in my case, the home directory), you can bring up the console (Figure 1-5) by typing:

```
$ java -jar ~/rhino.jar
```

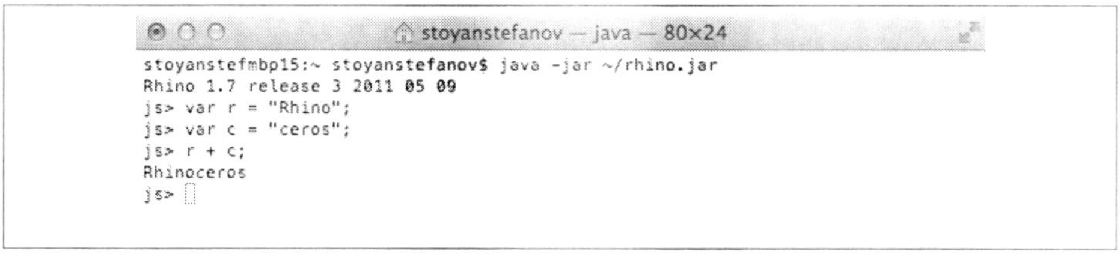

Figure 1-5. Rhino console

If you have a choice, use Node.js. You'll notice its REPL (read-evaluate-print loop) is similar to using php -a (if not better) for exploring and experimenting with the language.

Longer Examples

Using JavaScriptCore, Node.js, or Rhino, you can create longer examples and store them in separate files. In fact, this is how you can write your own shell scripts in JavaScript. You run external files by passing them as arguments:

```
$ jsc test.js
$ node test.js
$ java -jar ~/rhino.jar test.js
```

Let's Get Started

Armed with a handy JavaScript console, you're ready to embark on a journey in Java-Script land. To start, Chapter 2 examines JavaScript syntax, focusing on similarities with and differences from PHP.

JavaScript Syntax

Just like PHP, JavaScript has a C-like syntax, so you'll find it immediately familiar. This chapter goes over the basics, highlighting what's similar and what's different about variables, arrays, loops, conditions, and some miscellaneous (and slightly strange) operators.

Variables

To define a variable in PHP, you'd write:

```
// PHP
$n = 1;
```

The equivalent in JavaScript is:

```
// JavaScript
var n = 1;
```

There's no dollar sign, just the name of the variable. Like in PHP, you don't define variable types because the type is derived from the value. You use var for all types.

If you need a numeric type, you give your variable a numeric value. The same applies to booleans and strings:

```
var n = 1;        // number
var b = true;     // boolean
var s = "hello"; // string
```

You have the option of declaring a variable without initializing it with a value. In such cases, the variable is assigned the special value undefined:

```
var a;
a; // `a` has the special value `undefined`
```

Redeclaring an existing variable doesn't set the variable value back to `undefined`:

```
var a = 1;
var a;
// `a` is still 1
```

You can declare (and optionally initialize with a value) several variables with one `var` statement as long as you separate them with a comma and end with a semicolon:

```
var pi = 3.14,
    yeps = true,
    nopes,
    hi = "hello",
    wrrrld = "world";
```

Technically, `var` is optional. But unless the variable was defined higher up in the scope chain (discussed in more detail in Chapter 3), if you skip `var`, you end up with a global variable. And you've learned, probably the hard way, that global namespace pollution is a sin. Additionally, there are some subtle differences if you declare a global variable with and without `var`. To cut a long story short, resist this temptation and always use `var` to declare your variables.

Variables can be named using letters, numbers, underscore, and the dollar sign. You cannot start with a number, though:

```
var _1v; // Valid
var v1;  // Valid
var v_1; // Valid
var 1v;  // Invalid
```

What Does $ Do in JavaScript?

This is sort of a trick question sometimes asked at interviews. The short answer is: nothing.

You can name variables using $ anywhere in the name. Earlier ECMAScript standard editions recommended that $ should only be used in auto-generated code, a suggestion commonly ignored by developers. In reality, $ is often used as the name of a function that selects a DOM node in an HTML document.

Let's say you have this HTML markup:

```
<div id="myid"></div>
```

To get a reference to that DOM element, the DOM method `getElementById()` can be used:

```
var mydiv = document.getElementById("myid");
```

However, this is a lot of typing for something so commonly used in client-side programming. Thus, many libraries define a similar function, as follows:

```
function $(id) {
    return document.getElementById(id);
}
```

You can then do the following:

```
$("myid").innerHTML = "hello world";
```

The trick $ question lets the interviewer check if the candidate has any JavaScript experience outside of a specific library. Answering "$ selects a DOM element" is true for many libraries as well as browser consoles, but not for JavaScript itself.

 In most browser consoles, such as the Web Inspector and Firebug, the `$()` function exists for your convenience and quick access to DOM nodes. There's also `$$()`, which maps to `document.querySelectorAll()` and lets you find DOM elements by using a CSS selector, like so:

```
// List of <li> DOM nodes that are children of an element with ID "menu"
$$('#menu li');
```

Values

There are five primitive value types in JavaScript. Everything else is an object. The primitive types are:

- string
- boolean
- number
- null
- undefined

Anything between single or double quotes is a string value. Unlike PHP, there's no difference between single and double quotes.

The literals `true` and `false` without quotes create boolean values.

As far as numbers are concerned in JavaScript, there are no floats, ints, doubles, and so on; they are all numbers. You use a `.` to define a floating point value (e.g., `3.14`).

Prefixing the value with a 0 results in an octal value:

```
var a = 012;
a === 10; // true
```

 Octal literals are now deprecated and disallowed in "strict mode" in ES5.
(See Chapter 6 for more details on strict mode.)

Prefixing the value with a 0x gives you a hexadecimal value:

```
var a = 0xff;
a === 255;    // true
```

You can also use scientific notation:

```
var a = 5e3;  // 5 with three zeros
a === 5000;   // true

var b = 5E-3; // Moving the . three digits to the left of 5
b === 0.005;  // true
```

typeof Introspection

You can use the operator typeof to find the type of value you're working with:

```
var a = "test";
typeof a;      // "string"
typeof 0xff;   // "number"
typeof false;  // "boolean"
```

Sometimes typeof is used as a function (e.g., typeof(a)), but that's not really recommended. Remember that typeof is not a function, but an operator. The reason that typeof() works as a function is because in this context, () is also an operator, called a *grouping operator*, which is usually used to override operator precedence, as in:

```
3 * (2 + 1); // 9
// versus
3 * 2 + 1;   // 7
```

 JavaScript's typeof(a) is to typeof a as PHP's echo($a); is to echo
$a; (although for different reasons). Same for include($a) versus in
clude $a; in PHP. Even though it works, it's considered a bad practice
because it looks like something it is not.

null and undefined

So far, you've seen three of the five primitive types: string, boolean, and number. The other two are the types null and undefined.

The undefined type has only one value—the value undefined. When you declare a variable but do not initialize it, it's initialized with undefined. Also, when you have a function that doesn't return a value explicitly, it returns undefined:

```
var a;
typeof a; // "undefined"
var b = 1;
b = undefined;
typeof b; // "undefined"
```

Note that the typeof operator always returns a string. In the previous example, b has the value undefined, but typeof b returns the string "undefined". It's common for newcomers to confuse the string "undefined" and the value undefined. Consider these differences:

```
var b;
b === undefined;         // true
b === "undefined";       // false
typeof b === "undefined"; // true
typeof b === undefined;   // false
```

The null type has only one value—the value null. It's rarely useful, but can be passed in function calls when calling functions that take a lot of arguments or when you want to make an explicit differentiation between undeclared and uninitialized variables, since undefined may mean either of those.

Surprisingly, typeof returns "object" when used with a null value:

```
var a = null;
typeof a; // "object"
```

 You can expect typeof null to return "null" in one of the next versions of ECMAScript.

Arrays

In PHP, you define an array using:

```
// PHP
$a = array(1, 2, 3);
```

In JavaScript, you drop array and use square brackets:

```
// JavaScript
var a = [1, 2, 3];
```

 PHP version 5.4 adds support for short array syntax, so it becomes just like JavaScript:

```
// PHP
$a = [1, 2, 3];
```

These also work in JavaScript:

```
// JavaScript
var arr = Array(1, 2, 3);
var arrgh = new Array("a", "b", "c");
arr;   // [1, 2, 3]
arrgh; // ["a", "b", "c"]
```

There's more about this syntax later, but keep in mind that the square bracket notation (array literal) is preferred.

Just like in PHP, you can mix any type of values in an array, including other arrays:

```
// JavaScript
var a = [1, "yes", false, null, undefined, [1, 2, 3]];
```

Arrays in JavaScript are objects:

```
typeof a; // "object"
```

You'll find discussions of the properties and methods of array objects later in this book, but just to give you a flavor:

```
var a = [1, 2, 3];
a.length; // 3, like count() in PHP
```

Unfortunately, you cannot add an element using a[ ] as you do in PHP. You need to pass the index of the element you're adding:

```
a[3] = 4;
```

Or, more commonly, you use the length as the next index:

```
a[a.length] = "five";
```

Alternatively, there's the push( ) method, similar to PHP's array_push( ) function:

```
a.push(6);
```

The end result of executing all of these statements is:

```
a; // [1, 2, 3, 4, "five", 6]
```

You access elements using their index, just as you'd expect:

```
var b = a[4];
b; // "five"
```

Associative Arrays

There are no associative arrays in JavaScript. When you need one, use an object.

If you want to do this:

```
// PHP
$assoc = array('one' => 1, 'two' => 2);
```

in JavaScript, you'd write:

```
// JavaScript
var assoc = {'one': 1, 'two': 2};
```

So the difference is just about using : instead of => and wrapping the values in curly brackets {}.

The quotes around the keys—let's call them *properties* because they are indeed properties of an object—are commonly omitted. When the keys are valid identifiers (meaning they can be used as variable names), quotes are optional:

```
var assoc = {one: 1, two: 2};
```

Adding more to this associative array/object/dictionary:

```
assoc.three = 3;
```

To remove properties, use the delete operator:

```
delete assoc.two;
```

In ES3, there is no easy way to count the number of properties in an object other than going through all properties in a for-in loop. You'll see how in more detail later.

To access the properties of an object, use the *dot notation*:

```
assoc.one; // 1
```

Alternatively, use the *square bracket notation*, which looks more like an array in PHP:

```
assoc["one"]; // 1
```

Conditions

The if syntax is equivalent to the one in PHP:

```
var a, b;
if (a === "hello") {
  b = "world";
} else if (a === "goodbye") {
  b = "bye";
} else {
  b = "what?";
}
```

While PHP has several alternative syntax options for if-then-else control structures, in JavaScript, there's only one (not counting the ternary operator). Thus, you can't, for example, use `elseif` instead of `else if`.

Ternary Operator

The short conditional syntax known as a *ternary operator* (because it's an operator that takes three operands) looks familiar, too:

```
var num = 11;
var whatisit = (num % 2) ? "odd" : "even";
num + " is " + whatisit; // "11 is odd"
```

You've probably already learned to avoid stacking more than one ternary operator without parentheses, as it's tricky to read. Another reason is that it works differently in JavaScript. For example:

```
// PHP
echo true ? "a" : true ? "b" : "c"; // "b"

// Same as
echo (true ? "a" : true) ? "b" : "c"; // "b"
echo ("a"              ) ? "b" : "c"; // "b"
```

It's the same syntax in JavaScript, but with a different result, because of the different order of evaluation:

```
// JavaScript
true ? "a" : true ? "b" : "c"; // "a"

// Same as
true ? "a" : "I'm ignored"; // "a"
```

Strict Comparison

Have you noticed the triple equals sign === that all code examples used so far? Comparison works similar to PHP:

- Three equals signs mean *strict comparison* (the expressions are compared by both value and type).
- Two equals signs mean *loose comparison* (only values are compared and, if needed, one expression is cast to the type of the other to perform type comparison).

In order to make debugging easier, it's always preferable to know the types you're comparing, so using === is good practice. It's easier because you can catch errors while developing and before the program runs "in the wild" where values can be unpredictable. You also don't need to remember the casting rules and oddities, which are not exactly like those in PHP.

In general, there are a handful of *falsy* values (values that cast to `false` in nonstrict comparisons):

- Empty string `""`
- The number `0`
- The value `false`
- `null`
- `undefined`
- Special numeric value `NaN`, which means "not a number," like PHP's `NAN` constant

These might trip you in nonstrict comparisons:

```
null == undefined;  // true
"" == 0;            // true
```

but

```
null === undefined; // false
0 === "";           // false
```

because

```
typeof null === typeof undefined; // false, "object" !== "undefined"
typeof 0 === typeof "";           // false, "number" !== "string"
```

All objects are *truthy*. And since arrays are objects, they always cast to `true` in loose comparisons. This is different from PHP, where empty arrays are falsy:

```
// PHP
if (array()) {
  echo "hello";
  // Not reachable in PHP
}
// JavaScript
if ([]) {
  console.log('hello');
  // Reachable in JavaScript
}
```

Not all falsy values are nonstrict equal to one another:

```
undefined == null; // true
undefined == 0;    // false
```

To recap, you can make your life and the lives of those around you easier by always using strict comparison with ===. You don't need to remember the casting rules and their differences with PHP.

switch

The `switch` control statement works just like in PHP, with only one difference. The cases are evaluated using strict comparison:

```
// JavaScript
var a = "";
var result = "";

switch (a) {
case false:
  result = "a is false";
  break;
case a + "hello": // Expressions are allowed here
  result = "what?";
  break;
case "":         // Strict comparison
  result = "a is an empty string";
  break;
default:
  result = "@#$";
}
```

The result here is `"a is an empty string"`, where similar code in PHP would give you `"a is false"`.

try-catch

Try-catch blocks are also pretty much identical to PHP. Here's an example in PHP:

```
// PHP
try {
  throw new Exception('ouch');
} catch (Exception $e) {
  $msg = $e->getMessage();
}
```

And here it is in JavaScript:

```
// JavaScript
var msg = "";
try {
  throw new Error("ouch");
} catch (e) {
  msg = e.message;
}
msg; // "ouch"
```

The few noticeable differences are the following:

- An `Error` object is thrown, not an `Exception`
- Type is not declared when catching

- A `message` property is accessed as opposed to calling a `getMessage()` method

In JavaScript, there's also `finally` (which exists in PHP as well, since version 5.5.), but it is rare to see in practice, especially considering there are some bugs in IE with it:

```
var msg = "";
try {
  throw new Error("ouch");
} catch (e) {
  msg += e.message;
} finally {
  msg += " - finally";
}
msg; // "ouch - finally"
```

As you can see, the statements in the `finally` block are always executed, regardless of whether or not the `try` block threw an error.

> You'll see more about variable scope later, but note that the catch block is an exception to the rule, the rule being: no block scope, just function scope. In the example just shown, e is only visible inside the catch block. However, the error object e is the only exception; if you define other variables inside the catch block, they bleed outside of it:
>
> ```
> try {
>   throw new Error();
> } catch (e) {
>   var oops = 1;
> }
>
> typeof e;    // "undefined"
> typeof oops; // "number"
> ```

Try-catch has some performance implications when the `catch` block is executed, and should be avoided in performance-critical code paths (i.e., you should move it outside loops).

while and for Loops

The `while`, `do-while`, and `for` loops work exactly the same in JavaScript as PHP, both languages copying C syntax. Let's have some fun and take a look at an example that calculates the sum of the numbers from 1 to 100.

The code in this section runs in both languages, but in JavaScript, you should start with the following:

```
var $i, $sum;
```

It's not required, but emphasizes the good habit of always declaring your variables. If you skip this line, the code still works, but $i and $sum become global variables. The $ in front of the variable name is an uncommon but absolutely valid part of a name.

And here's the cross-language while loop example:

```
$i = 1;
$sum = 0;

while ($i <= 100) {
  $sum += $i++;
}

$sum; // 5050
$i;   // 101
```

$sum is now 5050.

Similarly, here's a cross-language example of a do-while loop:

```
$i = 1;
$sum = 0;

do {
  $sum += $i++;
} while ($i <= 100);

$sum; // 5050
```

The for loop is also the same in PHP, and the following example works in both languages as well:

```
$i = 1;
$sum = 0;

for ($i = 1, $sum = 0; $i <= 100; $i++) {
  $sum += $i;
}

$sum; // 5050
```

In all these examples, $i ends up being 101, not 100. Can you answer why?

for-in Loops

In JavaScript, when you need an associative array, you use an object. And you iterate over objects not in a foreach loop but in a for-in loop.

Let's say you have defined the following array in PHP:

```
// PHP
$clothes = array(
```

```
    'shirt' => 'black',
    'pants' => 'jeans',
    'shoes' => 'none', // Trailing comma OK, even recommended
);
```

The same data in JavaScript looks like this:

```
// JavaScript
var clothes = {
  shirt: 'black',
  pants: 'jeans',
  shoes: 'none' // Trailing comma not OK, because of old IEs
};
```

In PHP, you iterate over the data as follows:

```
// PHP
$out = '';
foreach ($clothes as $key => $value) {
  $out .= $key . ': ' . $value . '\n';
}
```

In JavaScript, you use the for-in loop:

```
// JavaScript
var out = '';
for (var key in clothes) {
  out += key + ': ' + clothes[key] + "\n";
}
```

You don't have direct access to the next property's value inside the loop, so you get the value by using the square bracket notation clothes[key].

Also note that the order in which the properties are enumerated is not guaranteed and depends on implementations. In other words, shoes may appear before shirt, although in the definition it's later. If you want to maintain the order, you need to use a regular array to store the data.

And just for illustration purposes, if you forget for a moment that in PHP you have access to => in foreach, you can do the following on PHP to mimic JavaScript's for-in:

```
$out = '';
foreach (array_keys($clothes) as $key) {
  $out .= $key . ': ' . $clothes[$key] . '\n';
}
```

Miscellaneous Operators

Before you dive into the important topic of functions, let's examine a few stranger JavaScript operators.

in

In the previous section, the `in` operator was used to iterate over the properties of an object. It can also be used to check whether a property exists in an object:

```
if ("shirt" in clothes) { // true
  // Do something
}

if ("hat" in clothes) {    // false

}
```

You can also do a check using the following:

```
if (clothes['shirt']) { // true
  // Do something
}
```

Or, more commonly, using the dot notation:

```
if (clothes.shirt) { // true
  // Do something
}
```

The difference is that `in` only tests for the presence of the property; it doesn't look at the value at all. Testing with `clothes.shirt` returns `true` only if the property exists *and* it has a non-falsy value.

As an example, if you add a new property:

```
clothes.jacket = undefined;
```

then:

```
"jacket" in clothes; // true
```

but:

```
!!clothes.jacket; // false
```

because `clothes.jacket` has the `undefined` value, which is falsy and casts to `false`.

This is similar to the difference between `isset()` and `!empty()` in PHP.

Alternatively, and more verbosely, you can check for presence but not value using the `typeof` operator:

```
typeof clothes.jacket !== "undefined" // true

// But watch out for false positives when a property is given `undefined` value
clothes.i_am_undefined = undefined;
typeof clothes.i_am_undefined === typeof clothes.i_dont_exist; // true
```

A shorter version of this is to compare to the undefined value:

```
clothes.jacket !== undefined // true
```

String Concatenation

When looking at the for-in loop example, you may have noticed that the + operator is used to concatenate strings:

```
var alphabet = "a" + "b" + "c";
alphabet; // "abc"
```

It may seem strange, but the + operator is used for both adding numbers as well as concatenating strings:

```
var numbers = "1" + "2" + "3";
var sum = 1 + 2 + 3;
numbers; // "123"
sum;     // 6
```

How do you know which operation will be performed? That depends on the type of the operands.

Needless to say, the + operator is a common source of errors, so it's important to keep the variable types in mind.

An alternative way to concatenate strings is to append to an array, and once done, join its elements. This concatenation even performs better in ancient IE versions (version 7 and earlier):

```
['R', 2, '-', 'D', 2].join(''); // "R2-D2"
```

And finally, there's also the concat() method for strings, which doesn't require you to create throwaway array objects just for concatenation:

```
"".concat('R', 2, '-', 'D', 2); // "R2-D2"
String.prototype.concat('R', 2, '-', 'D', 2); // "R2-D2"
```

Type Casting

Because + can do both addition and string concatenation, you can also use + to quickly change the types of variables:

```
+"1";    // Converts the string "1" to the number 1
"" + 1; // Converts the number 1 to the string "1"
```

Speaking of type casting, you can use !! to convert to a boolean:

```
!!1; // true
!!""; // false
```

The first ! negates and returns a boolean true if the value is falsy, and the second ! negates again to give you the desired result of converting to a boolean. Additionally, built-in constructors, which you'll see later in detail, can also be used to perform type casting:

```
Number("1") === 1;      // true
String(100) === "100"; // true
Boolean(0) === false;  // true
Boolean(100) === true; // true
```

void

Another operator you may come across is void. It takes any expression as an operand and returns undefined:

```
var a = void 1;
typeof a === "undefined"; // true
```

The void operator is rarely useful, but is sometimes used as an href in links. As with the typeof operator, people often misuse it together with the grouping operator () so it looks like a function call:

```
<!-- not a good practice -->
<a href="javascript:void(0)">click and nothing happens</a>
```

This bad practice looks innocent enough, but when you think about it, it's as silly as it is common. Here's what happens:

1. The user clicks, and a JavaScript expression is evaluated.

2. The literal value 0 is sent as an operand to the grouping operator ().

3. The grouping operator returns the last value in the group, 0.

4. 0 is now sent to the void operator.

5. void, being the black hole that it is, takes the operand and returns undefined.

Ignoring for a moment the broken semantics of having links that do nothing, people might just as well make the href be javascript:undefined.

Comma Operator

The comma operator is another slightly odd one. It's the lowest precedence operator in JavaScript. It simply returns the value of the last operand passed to it:

```
var a = ("hello", "there");
a; // "there"
var a = ("hello", "there", "young", "one");
a; // "one"
```

It's similar to && and ||, but while these stop evaluating the expression when the outcome is clear, the comma operator keeps going:

```
0 && 7 && 1; // 0
0 || 7 || 1; // 7
0, 7, 1;     // 1
```

The comma operator is useful when you want to sneak in another expression where JavaScript expects only one.

 Did you notice in the previous example that && and || don't always return a boolean as they do in PHP? They return the value of the appropriate expression instead. This may be a little confusing, especially in the following common pattern of dealing with defaults in JavaScript:

```
// JavaScript
var a = 100;
var b = a || 200;
b; // 100
```

```
// PHP
$a = 100;
$b = $a || 200;
var_dump($b); // bool(true)
```

CHAPTER 3

Functions

Functions are an important topic in JavaScript because the language has many uses for them. In their most basic form, they look like a PHP function:

```
// Works in both languages
function sum($a, $b) {
  return $a + $b;
}

sum(3, 5); // 8
```

Default Parameters

There's no syntax that allows you to have a default value of a function parameter, as is often done in PHP. This is scheduled for a future version of ECMAScript, but for now you have to take care of this yourself inside the body of your function. Let's say you want the second parameter to default to 2:

```
// PHP
function sum($a, $b = 2) {
  return $a + $b;
}
// JavaScript
function sum(a, b) {
  b = b || 2;
  // Also sometimes written as
  // b || (b = 2)
  return a + b;
}
```

This is a short syntax that works fine in many cases, but it's a little naive in this particular example because b || 2 is a loose comparison for b. If you pass 0 as an argument, the comparison evaluates to false and b becomes 2:

```
sum(3);    // 5
sum(3, 0); // 5, not what you'd expect
```

A longer version is to use `typeof`:

```
function sum(a, b) {
  b = typeof b === "undefined" ? 2 : b;
  return a + b;
}

sum(3, 0); // 3
sum(3);    // 5
```

Any Number of Arguments

You don't have to pass all the arguments that a function expects, and JavaScript won't complain. In other words, there are no required parameters. If you need to make a parameter required, you need to enforce this in the body of your function.

You can also pass more arguments than a function expects, and these are happily ignored without any errors:

```
sum();             // NaN (not a number)
sum(1, 2);         // 3
sum(1, 2, 100, 999); // 3
```

You can prepare for receiving any number of arguments and handle this case gracefully. In PHP, you can use `func_get_args()`, which returns an array of arguments passed to your function. In JavaScript, you use the `arguments` array-like object. It's an object available to your function's body. It's dubbed "array-like" because its properties are enumerated starting from index 0, and it also has a `length` property, just like an array:

```
function sum(/* nothing here */) {
  for (var i = 0, result = 0; i < arguments.length; i++) {
    result += arguments[i];
  }
  return result;
}

sum();             // 0
sum(111);          // 111
sum(1, 2);         // 3
sum(1, 2, 3);      // 6
sum(1, 10, 2, 9, 3, 8); // 33
```

Remember that although it looks like an array, `arguments` is in fact an object, and it doesn't have array methods such as `push()`, `pop()`, etc. However, you can easily convert this array-like object to an array. Brace yourself for something new that's related to `prototype`, which will be explained in detail later:

```
function sum() {
  var args = Array.prototype.slice.call(arguments);
  typeof arguments.push; // "undefined"
  typeof args.push;      // "function"
}
sum();
```

 The typeof operator returns the string "function" when used with
functions.

arguments.length Trick

A clever approach to handling optional parameters is the one suggested by Andrea
Giammarchi that uses the arguments object:

```
// Here you have a function with all four default
// parameters, mimicking PHP's declaration:
// function sum($a = 1, $b = 2, $c = 3, $d = 4) ...
function sum(a, b, c, d) {
  // Note: no `break` needed
  switch (arguments.length) {
    case 0: a = 1;
    case 1: b = 2;
    case 2: c = 3;
    case 3: d = 4;
  }
  return a + b + c + d;
}

// test
sum();          // 10
sum(1);         // 10
sum(11);        // 20
sum(1, 2, 3, 24); // 30
sum(11, 22);    // 40
```

Return Values

Functions always return a value. If the function doesn't use return, then the value
undefined is returned implicitly:

```
// Explicit `return`
function iReturn() {
  return 101;
}
iReturn() === 101;              // true
```

```
typeof iReturn() === "number";      // true

// Implicit `return`
function noReturn() {
// Nothing
}
noReturn() === undefined;           // true
typeof noReturn() === "undefined"; // true
```

Functions Are Objects

It's important to understand that functions in JavaScript are objects. They come with some properties and methods of their own.

For example, take a look at this simple function:

```
function sum(a, b) {
    return a + b;
}
```

The `length` property of a function object tells you how many formal parameters are listed in the `()` part of the function definition, or in other words, how many arguments the function expects:

```
sum.length; // 2
```

The methods `call()` and `apply()` of the function objects offer an alternative way to call the function:

```
sum.call(null, 3, 4);      // 7
sum.apply(null, [3, 4]); // 7
```

The difference between the two is that `apply()` takes the arguments to pass to the function as an array, as opposed to one by one. These two methods are similar to what you can do in PHP using the following:

```
// PHP
call_user_func('sum', 3, 4);
call_user_func_array('sum', array(3, 4));
```

The fact that functions are objects means that you can add properties and methods to the function objects. This can be useful, for example, to cache the results of a function invocation to avoid duplicate work.

 If you're wondering about the first parameter `null` passed to `call()` and `apply()`, you can ignore it for now. You'll find out more about it later. Spoiler: it's an object that the `sum()` function can refer to as `this` inside its body if it so desires.

A Different Syntax

Functions are objects, so they can be assigned to variables just like all other data types. The following snippet shows a perfectly valid and commonly used syntax:

```
var sum = function (a, b) {
  return a + b;
};

sum(2, 2); // 4
```

This syntax shows what is called a *function expression*, as opposed to the other syntax you're familiar with, which is called a *function declaration*. The function declaration is the more common syntax, and the only one available in PHP before version 5.3.

There's a semantic difference in the meaning of the `function` keyword depending on the context. In a function expression, it's an operator. In a function declaration, it's a statement.

Note the trailing semicolon in the function expression. Unlike function declarations, function expressions require a semicolon.

JavaScript has a semicolon insertion mechanism where the interpreter adds the semicolons for you if you forget them. However, it's always preferable to add the semicolons yourself to avoid ambiguities. It also proves helpful when you minify your code in order to reduce its size in production, because with minification, all the code is pretty much on one line.

There is one more syntax you may encounter called *named function expression* (NFE). It looks like this:

```
var sum = function plum(a, b) {
  return a + b;
};

sum(21, 21);  // 42
plum(21, 21); // Error: plum() is not defined
```

This sort of syntax can be helpful while debugging when the debugger reads the nonstandard but commonly available `name` property of the function object:

```
sum.name; // "plum"
```

This syntax is called a named function expression because you assign a name to the function. If you don't, which is much more common, you end up with an *unnamed function expression*, or simply called a *function expression* or an *anonymous function*.

Setting the name (identifier) of the expression to something other than the variable you assign it to (as with plum and sum in the preceding example) is *not* recommended. It's confusing to read, and in many IE versions, it mistakenly creates two symbols (variables) in the enclosing scope. In other words, typeof plum will be "undefined" in modern browsers and "function" in older IEs. So it's best to set the name matching to the variable you assign it to, like:

```
var sum = function sum(a, b) {
  return a + b;
};
```

This is useful for debugging and a good minifier should strip the name if it detects it's not used in the body of the function.

Scope

There's no block scope in JavaScript, only function scope.

Any variables you define inside of a function are local to the function and not visible outside it. Global variables are those defined outside of any function:

```
if (true) {
  // Global even if in a curly braces block
  var true_global = 1;
}

if (false) {
  var false_global = 1;
}

var sum = function () {
  var local = 1;
  is_it_local = 1;
  return true_global + local + is_it_local;
};

true_global;  // 1
false_global; // undefined
local;        // ReferenceError: local is not defined
is_it_local;  // ReferenceError: is_it_local is not defined

sum(); // 3

true_global;  // 1
false_global; // undefined
```

```
local;        // ReferenceError: local is not defined
is_it_local;  // 1
```

Things to note in the previous snippet:

- `true_global` is always available.

- Even inside of a nonexecuted block of code, `false_global` is always declared, although not initialized. Using it returns `undefined` (which is the default value for all variables), and is not an error.

- `local` is never available outside of the function `sum()`; it's local to the function. Trying to use it outside its local environment is an error.

- `is_it_local` was not declared before using the `sum()` function, and was causing an error. Calling `sum()` assigns a value to `is_it_local` and puts it in the global scope because of the missing `var` statement. This is something you should avoid in order to prevent global namespace pollution.

Some exceptions of the blanket statement "there's no block scope":

- Block scope is planned for the next version of ECMAScript by using `let` instead of `var`

- The error object in a `catch` block is scoped to its block:

```
try {
  throw new Error("Yuck!");
} catch (err) {
  err.message; // "Yuck!"
}
typeof err;    // "undefined"
```

Hoisting

When the program execution enters a new scope (e.g., in a new function, the global scope, or `eval()`), all the variables defined anywhere in the function are moved, or *hoisted*, to the top of the scope. This is something to be aware of, as it can be a little confusing:

```
var a = 1;
function hoistingTest() {
  console.log(a);
  var a = 2;
  console.log(a);
}

hoistingTest(); // Logs "undefined", then 2
```

You might expect that the first console.log() would see the global a value of 1. But instead, you get undefined because the declaration of the local a was hoisted to the top. Only the declaration was hoisted, but not the assignment to 2. It's as if the function was written like this:

```
function hoistingTest() {
  var a;
  console.log(a);
  a = 2;
  console.log(a);
}
```

To prevent confusion, many developers adopt the convention of always declaring all variables at the top, regardless of where they are used. This can be thought of as an annoying *manual hoisting* because, after all, that's just the way things work, and hoisting is the JavaScript interpreter's job. But it can make the code more explicit and easier to read. The other option—defining variables where you need them—results in *mental hoisting* you need to do every time you read a (potentially long) function:

```
function mine() {
  // Declare all, once at the top
  var a, b = 2, c = 3;

  // Use later, anywhere
  // ...
  a = b;
  // ...
  return c + a;
}
```

You can think of "single var goes at the top of the function" rule as similar to defining a PHP class and putting all properties at the top of the class, as opposed to sprinkled among the methods.

Hoisting Functions

Functions are just objects assigned to a variable, so it's to be expected that they are hoisted, too. There's a difference, though, depending on the way they were defined.

Consider the following example:

```
// Global scope
function declare() {}
var express = function () {};

(function () {
  // Local scope
  console.log(typeof declare); // "function"
  console.log(typeof express); // "undefined"

  function declare() {}
```

```
var express = function () {};

console.log(typeof declare); // "function"
console.log(typeof express); // "function"

}());
```

Both local functions declare() and express() are "shadowing" the global variables with the same names because they are hoisted to the top of the function, although they are defined later. But in the case of the function expression express(), only the var is hoisted while the function declaration (declare()) is hoisted together with its value (implementation). With hoisting in mind, the function acts as if written like so:

```
// Global scope
function declare() {}
var express = function () {};

(function () {
  // Local scope

  function declare() {}        // Declared and given a value
  var express = undefined;     // Declared here

  console.log(typeof declare); // "function"
  console.log(typeof express); // "undefined"

  express = function () {};    // Implemented here

  console.log(typeof declare); // "function"
  console.log(typeof express); // "function"

}());
```

Closures

A closure is a function together with its environment of nonlocal variables. In JavaScript, every function is a closure, so there's nothing special about closures—they are just functions. But you should understand the behavior of functions, because failing to do so will cause a lot of debugging headaches.

Closures in PHP

Closures exist in PHP, too, starting with PHP 5.3 (*http://php.net/manual/en/func tions.anonymous.php*).

You already know this common syntax to define a function in JavaScript using a function expression:

```
// JavaScript
var sum = function (a, b) {
```

```
    return a + b;
  };
```

And here's a similar syntax in PHP (version 5.3 and above):

```
// PHP
$sum = function ($a, $b) {
  return $a + $b;
};
$sum(9, 11); // 20
```

Unlike in JavaScript, PHP functions don't have automatic access to the global or parent environments. If you need to make a variable from the parent scope available inside the closure, you need to declare your intentions with use:

```
// PHP
$global_ten = 10;

function papa() {
  global $global_ten; // Localize the global
  $hundred_more = 100;
  $sum = function ($a, $b) use ($global_ten, $hundred_more){
    return $a + $b + $global_ten + $hundred_more;
  };
  return $sum(9, 11);
}

echo papa(); // 130
```

In JavaScript, use doesn't exist, and the behavior where the inner function has access to the variables of its environment is automatic:

```
// JavaScript
var global_ten = 10;

function papa() {
  var hundred_more = 100;
  var sum = function (a, b) {
    return a + b + global_ten + hundred_more;
  };
  return sum(9, 11);
}

papa(); // 130
```

papa() has access to the variables of the environment in which it was defined. In this case, it's the global environment and its global_ten variable.

sum() has access to the parent's papa() environment, so it can access hundred_more. Also, by extension, sum() can also see all the variables the parent can see, meaning sum() has access to global_ten, too.

These parent-child relationships form a chain you can call the *scope chain*.

In PHP, when you capture interesting variables with use, you have the option to pass them by reference or by value (as in the example). In JavaScript, you always have references to the variables in closure scope.

Scope Chain

Every time the JavaScript interpreter enters a new function, it looks around to see what local variables are available. It gathers those and puts them in a special *variables* object.

If there's another function defined inside the first and the interpreter enters its body, another *variables* object is created for the inner function. The inner function also gets a special *scope* property, which points to the *variables* object of the outer function. The outer function is where the inner function was defined, as if in a dictionary. That's why you hear the term "lexical" ("lexical definition" being synonymous with "dictionary definition") to highlight the difference between definition of a function and its execution. The *scope* property is set during the function definition, not execution.

The *variables* object and the *scope* property are invisible from the programmer's perspective, but the following snippets use __variables and __scope for illustration. (__scope is known as [[Scope]] in the ECMAScript specs.)

If your function is not defined inside another, it's in the global space (the global scope). This place in the Universe also has a *variables* object containing all the variables in the global scope. So the *scope* property of the global function will hold a reference to the global *variables* object.

Consider a global function:

```
var global_ten = 10;
// __variables object contains all global variables
// {
//    global_ten: 10,
//    papa: function () {...},
//    ... all other globals
// }

function papa() {
  var hundred_more = 100;
  // __variables object has {hundred_more: 100}
  // __scope proprerty points to the variable object of the outer
  // Lexical environment (in other words, the global __variables object)
}
```

Here's the relationship represented in a linked list:

```
papa.__scope -> global __variables
```

Let's take a look at the previous code sample again, this time with line numbers:

```
1. var global_ten = 10;
2.
3. function papa() {
4.    var hundred_more = 100;
5.    var sum = function (a, b) {
6.       return a + b + global_ten + hundred_more;
7.    };
8.    return sum(9, 11);
9. }
10.
11. papa(); // 130
```

Starting on line 1 (the program code), the interpreter has its hidden __variables object with all variables (e.g., global_ten and papa).

Because one of these is a function, it needs a __scope property. papa.__scope points to the global __variables.

Should the interpreter need to look up a variable's value, the lookup is really easy, because there's only one place to look:

```
[global __variables] global_ten, papa
```

Next thing you know, the interpreter is on line 11. It enters the function papa() and finds itself on line 4. It looks around and creates another __variables object that contains hundred_more and sum. You see now why hoisting is needed: the interpreter has to find all variables sprinkled throughout the function body and keep them handy in one place. Moving on to line 5, it turns out sum is also a function, so it needs a __scope property. Now sum.__scope should point to papa() __variables, as this is where sum() is lexically defined. The linked list (chain) of scopes becomes:

```
sum.__scope -> papa's __variables -> global __variables
```

Now if the interpreter needs to look up a variable, it looks in the local __variables of papa(). If the variable is not found, then the interpreter will follow this sequence: "OK, I'm inside the function papa(), and there's no local variable with that name. Let me see where papa.__scope points to. Oh, lookie, another __variables thing, full of more variables; I'd better check what's in there!"

```
[papa() local __variables] hundred_more, sum
[global __variables] global_ten, papa
```

Next, on line 8, the code calls sum(), so the interpreter enters this function and finds itself on line 6. There it creates yet another __variables object containing a and b. These are not declared with var but are declared by way of being used as the function's formal parameters.

What used to be a local scope now becomes a closure scope, as there's now another immediate local scope at hand:

```
[sum() local __variables] a, b
[papa() closure __variables] hundred_more, sum
[global __variables] global_ten, papa
```

When the interpreter has to perform the arithmetic operation on line 6, it starts looking for values to replace the variables. You can imagine the interpreter thinking something along these lines:

```
a // Got it in the [local] scope, we're good.
b // Also in the [local] scope, excellent.
global_ten // Hm, not in [local], let me dig deeper.
           // What's sum()'s __scope? I see, a [closure]!
           // Meh, not in [closure] either, let's keep going.
           // [closure] is papa()'s __variables object. So what's papa.__scope?
           // It's the [global __variables].
           // I found `global_ten` in [global] scope, yay me!
           // This was the last chance, otherwise I would
           // need to throw an error.
hundred_more // Not in [local], but found in [closure], all fine.
```

You see now how a chain (the scope chain) is created in the form of a linked list where each function knows its lexical __scope. When the interpreter needs a variable and doesn't find it locally, it starts following the chain of linked scopes, looking for that variable.

The Scope Chain in the WebKit Console

When debugging in the WebKit console (in either Chrome or Safari), you can look at the scope objects and what they contain. I've created an HTML file (*http://www.jspat terns.com/js4php/scope.html*) you can practice with. Here's how:

1. Load the file in a WebKit browser.

2. Right-click anywhere and select "Inspect element" to bring up the Web Inspector.

3. Click the Scripts tab.

4. Insert breakpoints by clicking on line numbers 8 and 21.

You should see see something like what is shown in Figure 3-1.

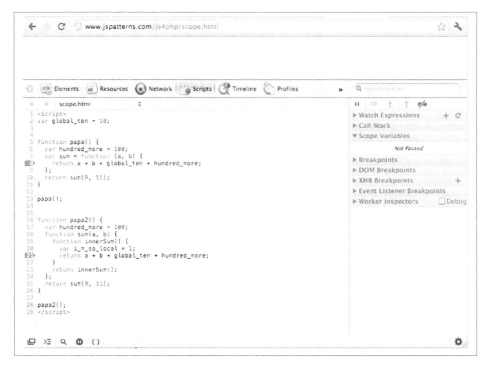

Figure 3-1. Breakpoints in the Web Inspector

Now refresh the page and you'll see the code execution stop at line 8. Look at the right-hand menu, in the Scope Variables section. You'll clearly see the chain consisting of Global, Closure, and Local sections, and the variables available inside (Figure 3-2).

Figure 3-2. Reaching the breakpoint in Chrome

The Global section is really big, but if you scroll down, you'll find the global_ten.

You might notice that sum is missing from the Closure in Figure 3-2. It should be there; it's just a question of displaying it in the Web Inspector in the version of Chrome this screenshot was taken with. If you do the same in Safari, you can see a different picture that includes sum and also the arguments object (Figure 3-3).

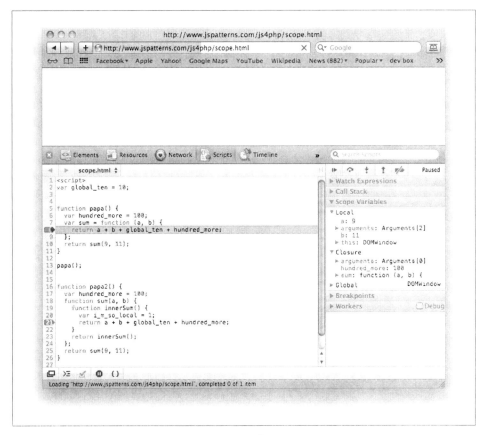

Figure 3-3. Reaching the first breakpoint in Safari

Now if you click the Play button in the debugger to continue execution, you'll reach the second breakpoint on line 21. It has two Closure sections in the scope list because the function innerSum() is defined inside sum() and it creates yet another link in the scope chain (Figure 3-4).

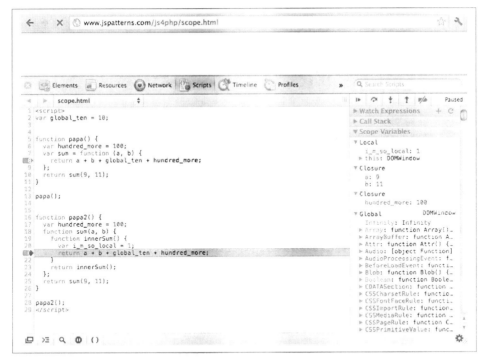

Figure 3-4. Reaching the second breakpoint

Retaining the Scope

As you know now, local functions have access to the scope of the environment where they were defined. When the execution moves out of a local function such as `inner Sum()` or `sum()`, the local scope of this function (its `__variables` object) is no longer available and can be destroyed and garbage collected unless there's someone who still needs it. This is interesting, and is as powerful as it is error prone.

Let's say that `sum()` wasn't a local function, but a global one. It is still defined in a local environment, but the variable `sum` was declared in the global scope:

```
var global_ten = 10;
var sum;

function papa() {
  var hundred_more = 100;
  sum = function (a, b) {
    return a + b + global_ten + hundred_more;
  };
  return sum(9, 11);
}

papa(); // 130
```

Now after `papa()` was called, you have a brand new `sum()` function available to call from the global scope. When you call `sum()`, it has access to all global variables such as `global_ten` (without special syntax such as PHP's `$GLOBAL`). But it also, maybe surprisingly, has access to `hundred_more` and can see its value:

```
sum(9, 11); // 130
```

What happened here? After `papa()` returns, what happens to its local scope? In the previous example, when `sum()` was local, then the local scope is just released, as no one needs it. But when `sum()` is global and it's defined in `papa()`, then `sum.__scope` refers to the local scope of `papa()`. Therefore, this scope needs to be retained for future use and cannot be destroyed. `sum.__scope` holds a reference to it.

This is important to understand and keep in mind about JavaScript closures (functions): they retain the referencing environment, which is the environment they were defined in and is also called the lexical environment.

The function `papa()` also retains its referencing environment, but it happens to be the global scope, which is always around anyway.

Retaining References, Not Values

It's also important to understand that only references to the environment are retained, not specific values. Let's see an example:

```
var global_ten = 10;
var sum;

function papa() {
  var hundred_more = 100;
  sum = function (a, b) {
    return a + b + global_ten + hundred_more;
  };
  hundred_more = 100000; // This is different from the previous example
}

papa();     // No explicit return value this time

sum(9, 11); // 100030
```

At the time `sum()` was defined, `hundred_more` had the value `100`, but later, it became `100000`. At the time `papa()` returns, its local scope was updated with the new `100000` value. This is the scope that `sum()` has access to. `sum()` will see the latest state of the referencing environment.

Note the difference with PHP when you "localize" a variable with use:

```
$hundred_more = 100;
$sum = function ($a, $b) use ($hundred_more) {
```

```
    return $a + $b + $hundred_more;
};
$hundred_more = 100000;
echo $sum(0, 0); // 100
```

The same thing in JavaScript returns 100,000 because only the reference to hun
dred_more would be retained, not its value:

```
var hundred_more = 100;
var sum = function (a, b) {
  return a + b + hundred_more;
};
hundred_more = 100000;
sum(0, 0); // 100000
```

Closures in a Loop

Let's see another example where this difference becomes even more obvious. Let's define
an array of functions:

```
var fns = [];

function definer() {
  for (var i = 0; i < 5; i++) {
    fns.push(function () {
      return i;
    });
  }
}

definer();
```

Here you loop from 0 to 4, defining five functions. You can call these functions like so:

```
fns[0]();
fns[1]();
fns[2]();
fns[3]();
fns[4]();
```

If you haven't read the previous section, you might naively think that each of these
function calls returns the value of i at the time of each function definition. But all the
five functions were defined in the same environment and have access to the same local
scope.

When definer() returns, i has the value 5, not 4, because at the last iteration there was
one final i++. This is the value that exists in the retained environment, and all five
functions see it. So all five functions return 5:

```
fns[0](); // 5
fns[1](); // 5
fns[2](); // 5
```

```
fns[3](); // 5
fns[4](); // 5
```

And what if you do want all functions to return an incremented value? You use another closure to "localize" the value of i into a local_i:

```
var fns = [];

function definer() {
  for (var i = 0; i < 5; i++) {
    fns.push(function (local_i) {
      return function () {
        return local_i;
      };
    }(i));
  }
}

definer();
```

Another scope object was introduced here. In this new scope, there's a local variable local_i. It's initialized with the current value of i and retained. In fact, now each of the five functions has its own environment, different from the other four.

This is now more like what you'd expect:

```
fns[0](); // 0
fns[1](); // 1
fns[2](); // 2
fns[3](); // 3
fns[4](); // 4
```

How about a small improvement: simplifying the loop inside definer()? You can introduce a utility binder() function that returns a new function with the local i value:

```
var fns = [];

function binder(i) {
  return function () {
    return i;
  };
}

function definer() {
  for (var i = 0; i < 5; i++) {
    fns.push(binder(i));
  }
}

definer();

// Test
fns[0](); // 0
```

```
fns[1](); // 1
fns[2](); // 2
fns[3](); // 3
fns[4](); // 4
```

Exercise: onclick Loop

Let's see a more practical example that demonstrates the same idea that referencing environment variables are retained by reference, not values.

Say you have three buttons on an HTML page with incrementing ID attributes:

```
<button id="button-1">one</button>
<button id="button-2">two</button>
<button id="button-3">three</button>
```

Then you assign click event handlers in a loop:

```
<script>
for (var i = 1; i <= 3; i++) {
  document.getElementById('button-' + i).onclick = function () {
    alert("This is button: " + i);
  };
}
</script>
```

Again, this code may look like it should work fine, but any button you click always gives you:

```
"This is button: 4"
```

You can play with the example online (*http://www.jspatterns.com/js4php/closure-dom-loop.html*).

As an exercise, think about how to modify the loop so that the three buttons return respectively:

```
This is button: 1
This is button: 2
This is button: 3
```

Immediate Functions

In the definer() function earlier, a bit of new syntax that wasn't mentioned previously was introduced: the trailing (). It instructs the interpreter to take the function that was just defined and execute it immediately:

```
var immediate_one = function () {
  return 1;
}();

immediate_one; // 1
```

Here you see a call to a one-off function that runs and returns a value, which you then assign to the variable immediate_one.

If the example were:

```
var immediate_one = function () {
    return 1;
};
```

then immediate_one would be a function, not the return value of a function invocation, and it wouldn't run, but be simply defined.

And how about this syntax?

```
// Syntax error
function myfunc() {
    return 1;
}();
```

This is not valid syntax because myfunc() was defined using the function declaration syntax, not the function expression syntax. The difference sometimes may not be noticeable unless you take into account *where* the code is in the program.

You can fix this syntax error by passing the function as an operand to the grouping operator:

```
// Valid syntax
(function myfunc() {
    return 1;
})();
```

All you need to do is wrap the function in parentheses. How is that different? Well, in this case, the function is no longer in the main program code, but is passed as an operand to an operator—the grouping operator ( )—which simply returns the function. This turns the function declaration into a function expression, and the ( ) that follows executes the function. Function declarations cannot be operands; therefore, the interpreter can disambiguate the syntax and treat this function as a function expression.

This is also a valid placement of the grouping operator's parentheses:

```
// Still valid syntax
(function myfunc() {
    return 1;
}());
```

Immediate functions are a useful and common construct to deal with the way variable scope works in JavaScript. Immediate functions are also sometimes called *self-executing* or *self-invoking* functions, although this is confusing, as it may mean a recursive function. They are also called IIFE (immediately-invoked function expressions), but that's a bit of a mouthful.

The grouping operator () is also commonly used even when not required, for readability. In the following example, `hardtoread` and `easytoread` both have value 1, but the presence of the opening (signals to the reader of the code that there is something going on here (otherwise, it's easy to confuse `hardtoread` to be a function and not the returned value of a function):

```
var hardtoread = function () {
  return 1;
}();

var easytoread = (function () {
  return 1;
})();

hardtoread === easytoread; // true
```

Initialization

One use for immediate functions is one-off initialization. Often, you want to do some initialization without leaving global variables behind. If this initialization is complex enough that it needs temporary variables, you can wrap all your initialization code in an immediate function to clean up after yourself.

The following code that assigns click event handlers to buttons is a good candidate:

```
(function () {
  for (var i = 1; i <= 3; i++) {
    document.getElementById('button-' + i).onclick = function () {
      // ...
    };
  }
}());
```

If there was no immediate function, the variable i would remain in the global scope.

As you can see, the function closes over variables used in the piece of code, hence the name *closure*.

Privacy

Immediate function are also often used to achieve privacy. You can have global functions that are defined in the closure of another function and share this closure's local scope.

Here's a simple iterator implementation:

```
var next, previous, rewind; // Globals

(function () {

  // Private data
  var index = -1;
```

```
        var data = ['eeny', 'meeny', 'miny', 'moe'];
        var count = data.length;

        next = function () {
          if (index < count) {
            index++;
          }
          return data[index];
        };

        previous = function () {
          if (index >= 0) {
            index--;
          }
          return data[index];
        };

        rewind = function () {
          index = -1;
        };

    }());
```

In this example index, data and count are private since the users of this iterator only need the methods to go back and forth, and probably shouldn't have access to the data and the pointer, should they decide to mess them up.

Testing going back and forth:

```
next();     // "eeny"
next();     // "meeny"
previous(); // "eeny"
```

More testing: rewind and start over:

```
var a;
rewind();
while (a = next()) {
  // Do something with `a`
}
```

Passing and Returning Functions

You already saw examples of passing functions around, but it's worth mentioning again: you can pass functions as arguments to other functions, and you can also have functions return other functions as their return values.

Previously, there was a function that returned a whole array of five functions. There's no reason why it cannot return just one function.

Functions are objects, and like any other objects, they can be passed as arguments. Here's an example that demonstrates all of this:

```
function goForIt(a, b, what) {
  return function () {
    return what(a, b);
  };
}
```

This function takes the parameter named what, which is expected to be a function. You could also call the function assigned to what a *callback function*. The goForIt() function returns a different (anonymous) function which in turn returns the result of executing the callback:

```
var sumOneAndTwo = goForIt(1, 2, function (one, two) {
  return one + two;
});
```

What is the value of sumOneAndTwo? It's not 3, but it's a function that returns 3:

```
sumOneAndTwo(); // 3
```

Note the line that executes the callback:

```
return what(a, b);
```

It can also be written as:

```
what.call(null, a, b);
```

or:

```
what.apply(null, [a, b]);
```

(You'll see more about the null argument in just a bit.)

You can define the callback function on the spot, like this:

```
var sumOneAndTwo = goForIt(1, 2, function (one, two) {
  return one + two;
});
```

This is just like you'd pass a closure as a callback in PHP.

But you can also reuse a different function you already have laying around:

```
function sum(a, b) {
  return a + b;
}

var mysum = goForIt(1, 99, sum);
mysum(); // 100

// Also
goForIt(1, 99, sum)(); // 100
```

Callbacks Are Not Strings

Note that you don't wrap the callback in quotes, meaning you don't pass it as a string:

```
// No-no
goForIt(11, 22, "sum")(); // TypeError: not a function
```

In the previous snippet, sum is a function object, not a string, so wrapping it in quotes means it will try to execute a string as a function, which won't work.

 In PHP, traditionally the callbacks were defined using function names as strings passed to call_user_func(), for example, but since the language has adopted closures, this is getting increasingly less common.

There are, however, some browser functions (e.g., setTimeout()) that accept callbacks, and are nice enough to deal with cases where people do pass a string.

Say you have this function that tells time:

```
function showTime() {
  alert(new Date());
}
```

You can schedule it to execute in 1 second (1,000 milliseconds):

```
setTimeout(showTime, 1000);
```

You can also see people doing things like this:

```
setTimeout("showTime()", 1000);
```

This works, too, but it feels wrong because you're expected to pass a function value, not a string. It works because setTimeout() checks what you're passing, and if it's a string, evaluates it. A sample implementation would be roughly something like this:

```
function setTimeout(callback, when) {

  // ... when the time is right ...

  if (typeof callback === "string") {
    (function () {
      eval(callback);
    }());
  } else {
    callback();
  }
}
```

To sum up, you pass the function value as a callback without quotes and without ()
because you're not executing the function at the time of passing it; you want it called
back later, when it's appropriate.

Last note: did you notice you can execute a function returned by another function
immediately by adding parentheses?

```
goForIt(11, 22, sum)(); // 33
```

CHAPTER 4

Object-Oriented Programming

This chapter discusses the object-oriented features of JavaScript, including objects, constructor functions, and prototypes. It also talks about code reuse and inheritance.

Constructors and Classes

In PHP, if you have a Dog class, you create a $fido instance of this class using:

```
// PHP
$fido = new Dog();
```

JavaScript has a similar syntax:

```
// JavaScript
var fido = new Dog();
```

One important difference is that Dog is not a class in JavaScript because there are no classes in the language. Dog is just a function. But functions that are meant to create objects are called *constructor functions*.

Syntactically, there is no difference between a regular function and a constructor function. The difference is in the intent. Thus, for readability purposes, it's a common convention to capitalize the first letter in constructor function names.

When you call a function with the new operator, it always returns an object. The object is known as this inside the body of the function. That's what happens even if you don't do anything special in the function. Remember that otherwise (when called without new) every function without an explicit return returns undefined:

```
function Dog() {
  this.name = "Fido";
  this.sayName = function () {
    return "Woof! " + this.name;
  };
```

```
}

var fido = new Dog();
fido.sayName(); // "Woof! Fido"
```

 In JavaScript, just as in PHP, parentheses are optional when you're not
passing arguments to the constructor, so this is also valid: `var fido =
new Dog;`

If you type `fido` in the console, you'll see that it has two properties: `name` and `sayName`.
Some consoles also show you a special property called __proto__, but you can ignore
it for now.

Take a look at the `sayName` property. It points to a function. Since functions are objects
in JavaScript, they can be assigned to properties, in which case you can also call them
methods. There's really no difference between properties and methods in JavaScript.
Methods are just callable properties.

Returning Objects

When you call any function with `new`, the following happens:

1. An "empty" object referenced via `this` is created automatically behind the scenes:

    ```
    var this = {}; // Pseudocode, would be a syntax error if you use it
    ```

2. The programmer adds properties to `this` at will:

    ```
    this.name = "Fido";
    ```

3. `this` is implicitly returned at the end of the function:

    ```
    return this; // Not an error, but you don't need to use it
    ```

The programmer can interfere with step 3 by returning a different object:

```
function Dog() {
  var notthis = {
    noname: "Anonymous"
  };
  this.name = "Fido";
  return notthis;
}

var fido = new Dog();
fido.name;   // undefined
fido.noname; // "Anonymous"
```

In this example, whatever you add to this is simply destroyed when the function returns. You might as well remove it, in which case you don't really need the magic provided by new and you can call the function as a regular function and achieve the same effect:

```
function Dog() {
  return {
    noname: "Anonymous"
  };
}

var fido = Dog(); // No `new` but `()` is needed this time
fido.name;        // undefined
fido.noname;      // "Anonymous"
```

Note, however, that returning something other than this causes the instanceof operator and the constructor property to not work as expected:

```
function Dog() {
  return {
    noname: "Anonymous"
  };
}

var fido = new Dog();
fido instanceof Dog;        // false
fido.constructor === Object; // true
```

When you use new you can return a custom object (not this), but it has to be an object. Trying to return a nonobject (a scalar value) results in your return value being ignored, and you still get this at the end:

```
function Dog() {
  this.name = "Fido";
  return 1;
}

var fido = new Dog();
typeof fido; // "object"
fido.name;   // "Fido"
```

More on This

As you know now, there's no difference between constructor functions and regular functions other than their usage intent. So what happens if you add properties to this in a nonconstructor function? In other words, what happens when you call a constructor function (which adds to this) and forget to call it with new?

```
function Dog() {
  this.thisIsTheName = "Fido";
  return 1;
```

```
}

var fido = new Dog();
var one = Dog();

// fido is a regular object:
typeof fido;        // "object"
fido.thisIsTheName; // "Fido"

// one is 1, as returned from a nonconstructor function
typeof one;         // "number"
one.thisIsTheName;  // undefined

// What?!
thisIsTheName;      // "Fido"
```

The surprise here is that by calling Dog() without new, the global variable thisIsThe Name gets created. That's because skipping new means this is a regular function invocation and now this refers to the global object. And properties added to the global object can be used as global variables. (There's more about the global object later.)

This is dangerous behavior because you don't want to pollute the global namespace. That's why it's important to use new when it's meant to be used. It's also important to follow the convention of naming constructors with a capital letter so you send a hint about their intended purpose to the reader of the code:

```
function Request() {} // Ahaa!, it's a constructor
function request() {} // Just a function
```

 This dangerous behavior is fixed in ECMAScript 5's strict mode.

Enforcing Constructors

If you are extra paranoid, you can make sure programmatically that your constructors always behave as constructors even when the callers forget new. You can use the instan ceof operator, which takes an object and a constructor function reference and returns true or false:

```
fido instanceof Dog; // true
```

Here's one way to implement the self-enforcing constructor:

```
function Dog() {

  // Check if the caller forgot `new`
  if (!(this instanceof Dog)) {
    return new Dog(); // Re-call properly
```

```
  }

  // Real work starts...
  this.thisIsTheName = "Fido";
  // real work ends

  // Implicitly at the end ...
  // return this;
}

var newfido = new Dog();
var fido = Dog();

newfido.thisIsTheName; // "Fido"
fido.thisIsTheName;    // "Fido"
```

The line `this instanceof Dog` checks if the newly created `this` object was created by Dog. The line `var fido = Dog();` didn't use new, so `this` points to the global object. The global object was definitely not created by Dog. After all, it was around even before Dog, so the check fails and the line `return new Dog();` is reached.

 You don't really know exactly which constructor was used to create the global object because it's an internal implementation dependent on the environment.

Another way to introspect and ask "Who created you?" is to use the `constructor` property that all objects have. It's also a writable property, so it's not really reliable, as the following example shows:

```
function Dog() {}
var fido = new Dog();

fido.constructor === Dog; // true, as expected
fido.constructor = "I like potatoes";
fido.constructor === Dog; // false, ... wait, what?!
fido.constructor;         // "I like potatoes"
```

Prototypes

The concept of *prototypes* doesn't exist in PHP but is an important concept in JavaScript.

Let's take a look at an example:

```
function Dog(name) { // Constructor
  this.name = name;
}

// Add a member to the `prototype` property
```

```
Dog.prototype.sayName = function () {
  return this.name;
};

var fido = new Dog("Fluffy");
fido.sayName(); // "Fluffy"
```

What happened here?

1. There's a normal function Dog, obviously created with the intent to be a constructor function because it starts with a capital D and refers to this inside its body.

2. Behind the scenes, the Dog() function, like any other function, automatically gets a property called prototype. (You know that functions are objects, so they can have properties.) The prototype property is always created for each function, constructor or otherwise.

3. You add a new property to the prototype property, called sayName. This property happens to be a function, so you can say it's a method.

4. sayName() has access to this.

5. Creating a fido object with new Dog() gives fido access to all the properties added to the prototype property. Otherwise, if you call Dog() without new, the proto type and everything in it is ignored.

6. fido.sayName() works fine even though sayName is not a property of the fido object.

An object can access properties and methods that don't belong to it but instead to the object referred to as prototype of the constructor function that created the object.

Let this sink in a bit; there's more on prototypes coming up.

Object Literals

You've already seen the use of object literals at several occasions in this book (e.g., when talking about representing PHP's associative arrays in JavaScript).

Object literals are simply key-value pairs, delimited with commas and wrapped in curly braces:

```
var obj = {
  name: "Fluffy",
  legs: 4,
  tail: 1
};
```

It's not OK to leave the trailing comma after the last property because some environments (earlier Internet Explorer versions) cannot handle it and raise an error.

You can also start with some properties (or no properties at all) and add more later:

```
var obj = {};
obj.name = "Fluffy";
obj.legs = 4;
obj.tail = 1;
```

Accessing Properties

Having created an object using the object literal notation, you can access the properties using the *dot notation*:

```
var desc = obj.name + " has " + obj.legs + " legs and " + obj.tail + " tail(s)";

desc; // "Fluffy has 4 legs and 1 tail(s)"
```

Alternatively, you can use the *square bracket notation* to access properties:

```
var desc = obj["name"] + " has " + obj["legs"] + " legs and " +
           obj["tail"] + " tail(s)";

desc; // "Fluffy has 4 legs and 1 tail(s)"
```

This is not too common, because it's longer and a little clumsy to be passing property names as strings. However, it is useful when you don't know the property name in advance and need a variable. For example, when iterating over all properties:

```
var all = [];
for (var property in obj) {
  all.push(property + ": " + obj[property]);
}
var desc = all.join(', ');

desc; // "name: Fluffy, legs: 4, tail: 1"
```

Or, as another example, when the property name is evaluated at runtime:

```
var obj = {
  foo: "Foo",
  bar: "Bar",
  foobar: "Foo + Bar = BFF"
};

var fprop = "foo", bprop = "bar";

obj[fprop];          // "Foo"
```

```
obj[bprop];            // "Bar"
obj[fprop + bprop]; // "Foo + Bar = BFF"
```

Square bracket notation is required when the property is not a valid identifier (same for quotes around property names in an object literal):

```
var fido = {};
fido.number-of-paws = 4;       // ReferenceError
fido['number-of-paws'] = 4; // This is OK
```

Confusing Dots

Dots in JavaScript are used to access properties, but in PHP, they concatenate strings. When you're mentally in PHP mode but you're writing in JavaScript, you can often confuse the purpose of the dot out of habit:

```
// JavaScript
var world = "wrrrld";
var result = "hello " . world;
```

Funny enough, this is not a syntax error in JavaScript. The result contains the value undefined. This is because the space around the dot is optional, so it works like this:

```
"hello".world; // undefined
```

In other words, you're accessing the property world of the string object "hello". String literals are converted to objects behind the scenes, as if you did new String("hel lo") (more about this coming soon). Since this object doesn't have such a property, the result is undefined.

Methods in Object Literals

Can you add methods to an object using object literal notation? Absolutely—methods are just properties, which happen to point to function objects:

```
var obj = {
  name: "Fluffy",
  legs: 4,
  tail: 1,
  getDescription: function () {
    return obj.name + " has " + obj.legs + " legs and " + obj.tail + " tail(s)";
  }
};

obj.getDescription(); // "Fluffy has 4 legs and 1 tail(s)"
```

 In getDescription(), you can substitute obj with this.

You can add methods to an existing object at a later time:

```
obj.getAllProps = function () {
  var all = [];
  for (var property in obj) {
    if (typeof obj[property] !== "function") {
      all.push(property + ": " + obj[property]);
    }
  }
  return all.join(', ');
};

obj.getAllProps(); // "name: Fluffy, legs: 4, tail: 1"
```

Did you notice some properties were filtered out using the following?

```
typeof obj[property] !== "function"
```

Most likely, you don't want functions showing up in the list of properties, but because functions are just like all other properties, they will show up if you don't filter them out. You can try removing this filter to see what happens.

 Spoiler alert: accessing a function object in a string concatenation context converts the function object to a string. This happens by calling the toString() method, which all objects that inherit Object respond to. Function objects implement toString() by returning the source code of the function, although this is not standard and implementations vary among engines in terms of new lines and spacing.

Fancy Arrays

Overall, the obj now looks like a fancy array, or like a PHP associative array that has some of its properties acting as functions. In fact, early PHP versions didn't have the concept of objects at all. When objects were added later, they were dubbed *fancy arrays*. To this day, it's easy to go back and forth between an object and an associative array in PHP:

```
// PHP
$mutt = array(
  'name' => "Fluffy",
  'legs' => 4,
  'tail' => 1,
);

echo $mutt['name'];     // "Fluffy"
var_dump($mutt->name); // NULL, this is not an object
```

Here $mutt is an array, so accessing `name` as a property doesn't work. However, you can convert $mutt to an object:

```php
// PHP
$mutt = (object)$mutt; // $mutt is now an object
echo $mutt['name'];    // Fatal error, this is not an array anymore
echo $mutt->name;      // "Fluffy"
```

As you can see, associative arrays and objects are so close that JavaScript decided to go with using only objects to express both concepts.

To continue the PHP/JavaScript analogy, you can imagine JavaScript's object literals as being associative arrays converted to objects behind the scenes. Just as if you do the following in PHP:

```php
// PHP
$mutt = (object)array(
  "name" => "Fluffy"
);

echo $mutt->name; // "Fluffy"
```

The same in JavaScript:

```javascript
// JavaScript
var mutt = {
  name: "Fluffy"
};

mutt.name; // "Fluffy"
```

Own Properties

In JavaScript, there is a distinction between properties owned by an object and properties that are inherited from a `prototype` object. The syntax for accessing either of those is the same, but sometimes you need to know if a property belongs to your object or if it came from someplace else.

Own properties are those added to an object using the object literal notation or via an assignment:

```javascript
var literal = {
  mine: "I pwn you"
};

literal.mine; // "I pwn you"

var assigned = {};
assigned.mine = "I pwn you";
```

Own properties are also those added to `this` and returned by constructor functions:

```
function Builder(what) {
  this.mine = what;
}

var constructed = new Builder("pwned");
constructed.mine; // "pwned"
```

Notice, however, that these two objects have access to a toString() method that neither of them defined:

```
literal.toString();     // "[object Object]"
constructed.toString(); // "[object Object]"
```

The method toString() is not an own method for either of the two objects. It's something that came from a prototype.

If you want to tell the difference between own properties and prototype properties, you can use another method called hasOwnProperty(), which takes a name of a property/method as a string:

```
literal.hasOwnProperty('mine');           // true
constructed.hasOwnProperty('mine');       // true
literal.hasOwnProperty('toString');       // false
constructed.hasOwnProperty('toString');   // false

literal.hasOwnProperty('hasOwnProperty'); // false
```

Let's do some more introspection. Where did that toString() come from? How can you find out which is the prototype?

__proto__

Objects have prototypes, but they don't have a prototype property—only functions do. However, many environments offer a special __proto__ property for each object. __proto__ is not available everywhere, so it's useful only for debugging and learning.

__proto__ is a property that exposes the secret link between the object and the prototype property of the constructor that created the object:

```
constructed.prototype; // undefined, objects don't have this property
constructed.constructor === Builder; // true, "who's your constructor?"

// Secret link - exposed!
constructed.constructor.prototype === constructed.__proto__; // true
```

Chaining __proto__ calls lets you get to the bottom of things. And the bottom is the built-in Object() constructor function.

Object.prototype is the mother of all objects. All objects inherit from it. That's where toString() was defined:

```
Object.prototype.hasOwnProperty('toString'); // true
```

You can trace down `toString` from the `constructed` object:

```
constructed.__proto__.__proto__.hasOwnProperty('toString'); // true
```

What about the `literal` object? Its chain is one link shorter:

```
literal.__proto__.hasOwnProperty('toString'); // true
```

This is because `literal` wasn't created by a custom constructor, which means it was created by `Object()` behind the scenes, not by something (e.g., `Builder()`) that inherits from `Object()`.

When you need a simple object temporarily, you can use (`{}`), and the following syntax also works:

```
({}).__proto__.hasOwnProperty('toString'); // true
```

 It was previously mentioned that object literals like var o = {} create "empty" objects. The word "empty" is in quotes because the objects are not really empty or blank. Every object, even if it doesn't have any own properties, has some properties and methods already available—the ones that come from its prototype chain.

this or prototype

When using constructor functions, you can add properties to `this` or to the constructor's `prototype`. You may be wondering which one you should use.

Adding to the `prototype` is more efficient and takes less memory because the properties and functions are created only once and reused by all objects created with the same constructor. Anything you add to `this` will be created every time you instantiate a new object.

Therefore, any members you plan to reuse and share among instances should be added to the `prototype`, and any properties that have different values in each instance should be own properties added to `this`. Most commonly, methods go to the prototype and properties to `this`, unless they are constant among the instances.

And talking about code reuse brings about the following question: Can you reuse code using inheritance?

Inheritance

So far you have learned:

- How to create objects with literal notation or with constructor functions
- What a prototype is (a property of each function)
- Own versus prototype properties
- Objects inherit properties from their prototypes and their prototypes' prototypes, and so on

Now let's talk a bit more about inheritance, because you're probably wondering how do inheritance works in a language that doesn't have classes. It turns out there's more than one option to implement inheritance, depending on your goals and preferences.

Inheritance via the Prototype

The default way to implement inheritance is to use prototypes. You create one object using a parent constructor and set it as a prototype of the child constructor.

Here's a constructor function that will be the parent:

```
function NormalObject() {
  this.name = 'normal';
  this.getName = function () {
    return this.name;
  };
}
```

And a second constructor:

```
function PreciousObject() {
  this.shiny = true;
  this.round = true;
}
```

And the inheritance part:

```
PreciousObject.prototype = new NormalObject();
```

Voila! Now you can create precious objects with all the functionality of the normal objects:

```
var crystal_ball = new PreciousObject();
crystal_ball.name = 'Ball, Crystal Ball.';
crystal_ball.round;      // true
crystal_ball.getName(); // "Ball, Crystal Ball."
```

Instead of the usual `Car extends Vehicle`, the examples in this chapter are inspired by Jim Bumgardner's blog post "Theory of the Precious Object" (*http://krazydad.com/blog/2008/07/31/theory-of-the-precious-object/*). It's a fun read that suggests that treasured objects, such as J. R. R. Tolkien's fictional One Ring or an iPhone, have certain common qualities.

Notice how you need to create an object with `new NormalObject()` and assign it to the `prototype` property of the `PreciousObject` function because the prototype is just an object. If you think in terms of classes, you know that a class inherits from another. And if you carry that thought to JavaScript, you'd expect that a constructor inherits from a constructor. But that's not the case. In JavaScript, you inherit an object.

If you have several constructor functions that inherit `NormalObject` objects, you may create `new NormalObject()` every time, but it's not necessary. You can create one normal object and reuse it as a prototype of the children. Even the whole `NormalObject` constructor may not be needed to begin with. Since you inherit an object, all you need is one object, regardless of how it's created.

Another way to do the same is to create one (singleton) normal object using the object literal notation and use it as a base for the other objects:

```
var normal = {
  name: 'normal',
  getName: function () {
    return this.name;
  }
};
```

Then the objects created by `PreciousObject()` can inherit `normal` like this:

```
PreciousObject.prototype = normal;
```

Inheritance via Copying Properties

Since inheritance is all about reusing code, another way to implement it is to simply copy over properties from one object to another.

Imagine you have these objects:

```
var shiny = {
  shiny: true,
  round: true
};

var normal = {
  name: 'name me',
  getName: function () {
    return this.name;
```

```
    }
};
```

How can `shiny` get the properties of `normal`? Here's a simple `extend()` function that loops through and copies properties:

```
function extend(parent, child) {
  for (var i in parent) {
    if (parent.hasOwnProperty(i)) {
      child[i] = parent[i];
    }
  }
}
```

```
extend(normal, shiny); // Inherit
shiny.getName();        // "name me"
```

Copying properties may look like overhead and something that can hurt performance, but for many tasks it's just fine. You can also see that this is an easy way to implement mixins and multiple inheritance.

 With this pattern, `instanceof` and `isPrototypeOf()` do not work as expected.

Beget Object

Douglas Crockford, a JavaScript luminary and creator of JSON, popularized another way to implement inheritance by using a temporary constructor just to be able to set its prototype:

```
function begetObject(o) {
  function F() {}
  F.prototype = o;
  return new F();
}
```

You create a new object, but instead of starting fresh, you inherit some functionality from another, already existing, object.

For example, say you have the following parent object:

```
var normal = {
  name: 'name me',
  getName: function () {
    return this.name;
  }
};
```

You can then have a new object that inherits from the parent:

```
var shiny = begetObject(normal);
```

The new object can be augmented with additional functionality:

```
shiny.round = true;
shiny.preciousness = true;
```

As you can see, there's no property copying, nor any constructors in sight. A new object inherits from an existing one. This was actually embraced by the community as a good idea, and is now part of ECMAScript 5 in the form of Object.create(), as you'll see in Chapter 6.

As an exercise in closures and optimization, can you change begetObject() so that F() is not created every time?

"Classical" extend()

Let's wrap up with yet another way to implement inheritance, which is probably the closest to PHP because it looks like a constructor function inheriting from another constructor function; hence, it looks a bit like a class inheriting from a class.

Here's the gist:

```
function extend(Child, Parent) {
    var F = function () {};
    F.prototype = Parent.prototype;
    Child.prototype = new F();
}
```

With this method, you pass two constructor functions to extend(). After extend() is done, any new objects created with the first constructor (the child) get all the properties and methods of the second (the parent) via the prototype property.

 This method is often referred to as "classical" in quotes because it looks the closest to the idea of classes.

There are only two small things to add to extend():

1. Have the child keep a reference to the parent, just in case.

2. Reset the constructor property of the child to point to the child's constructor, in case this is needed for introspection (you'll see some more about this property in Chapter 5):

```
function extend(Child, Parent) {
    var F = function () {};
    F.prototype = Parent.prototype;
```

```
    Child.prototype = new F();
    Child.prototype.parent = Parent;
    Child.prototype.constructor = Child;
}
```

In this method, there's no instance of new Parent() involved. This means that own properties added to this inside the parent constructor will not be inherited. Only the properties added to the prototype of the parent will be inherited. And this is OK in many scenarios. In general, you add the properties you want to reuse to the prototype.

Consider this setup:

```
function Parent() {
    this.name = "Papa";
}
Parent.prototype.family = "Bear";
function Child() {}
extend(Child, Parent);
```

The property name is not inherited, but the family is:

```
new Child().name;   // undefined
new Child().family; // "Bear"
```

And the child has access to the parent:

```
Child.prototype.parent === Parent; // true
```

Borrowing Methods

Using call() and apply() gives you an opportunity to reuse code without having to deal with inheritance at all. After all, inheritance is meant to help us reuse code.

If you see a method you like, you can temporarily borrow it, passing your own object to be bound to this:

```
var object = {
  name: "normal",
  sayName: function () {
    return "My name is " + this.name;
  }
};

var precious = {
  shiny: true,
  name: "iPhone"
};
```

If precious wants to benefit from object.sayName() without extending anything, it can simply do the following:

```
object.sayName.call(precious); // "My name is iPhone"
```

If you combine method borrowing and classical inheritance, you can also get both own and `prototype` properties:

```
function Parent(name) {
  this.name = name;
}
Parent.prototype.family = "Bear";

function Child() {
  Child.prototype.parent.apply(this, arguments);
}

extend(Child, Parent);
```

All `this` properties become own properties of the child. And via the magic of `argu ments` and `apply()`, you can also have arguments passed to the constructors, if you so desire:

```
var bear = new Child("Cub");
bear.name; // "Cub"
bear.family; // "Bear"
bear.hasOwnProperty('name'); // true
bear.hasOwnProperty('family'); // false
```

Conclusion

As you can see, there are many options available for implementing inheritance. You can pick and choose depending on the task at hand, personal preferences, or team preferences. You can even build your own solution or use one that comes with your library of choice. Note, however, that deep inheritance chains are not too common in JavaScript projects because the language allows you to simply copy properties and methods of other objects or "borrow" them to achieve your task. Or, as the Gang of Four's *Design Patterns* (Addison-Wesley, 1994) says: "Prefer object composition to class inheritance."

CHAPTER 5

The Built-In API

JavaScript has a small built-in API, and this chapter takes a look at pretty much all of it. There are only three global properties, nine global functions, and a handful of global objects, most of which are constructor functions. Most of the useful stuff is in the prototypes of the constructors or directly as properties of the constructors.

The Global Object

You already know about the global object, but let's revisit it. Each JavaScript environment has a global object, something like the $GLOBALS array in PHP.

Some environments, but not all, have a global variable that refers to the global object. Browsers call it window. You can access it using this in global program code or in a function, as long as the function is not called with new and you're not in ES5 strict mode —more on this later.

You can also think of global variables as being properties of the global object, with the only difference that you cannot delete them. Try the following in a browser:

```
// Create a global variable
var john = "Jo";
john;        // "Jo"
window.john; // "Jo", works as a property too

// Create a property of the global object
window.jane = "JJ";
jane;        // "JJ", works as a variable too
window.jane; // "JJ"

// Delete them
delete window.john; // false
delete window.jane; // true
```

```
john; // "Jo"
jane; // undefined

this === window; // true
```

 When you see BOM properties used with window.something, you can shorten them to just something (e.g., window.navigator is the same as navigator). Unless, of course, you have a local variable with the same name.

Global Properties

There are three built-in properties of the global object:

- NaN is a special value you get as a result of a math operation gone wrong:

  ```
  1 * 'a'; // NaN
  ```

- Infinity is what you get when you divide by 0:

  ```
  1 / 0; // Infinity
  ```

- And you already know about undefined.

The fact that these three special values are properties of the global object is of little interest. But a curious problem exists in ES3 (fixed in ES5)—you can overwrite them (e.g., Infinity = 1). This is, of course, a terrible idea, but it happens "in the wild." Here's a pattern that libraries adopt to prevent people from shooting themselves in the foot:

```
// Global program code
(function(window, undefined) {
    // window and undefined are what they should be

    // ... library goes here ...

}(this /*, no second parameter */));
```

Global Functions

There are nine global functions (four of these are related to numbers, another four are related to encoding/decoding URLs, and then there's eval()). Just like in PHP, eval() takes a string and evaluates it as code. Unfortunately, it's commonly used in dangerous and insecure ways, while the truth is that it's rarely needed.

Numbers

The four number-related functions are the following:

isNaN()
: Tells you if the argument is the NaN value. PHP has is_nan().

isFinite()
: Tells you if the argument is *not* the Infinity value. PHP has similar is_finite().

parseInt()
: Takes a string and returns an integer value, similar to intval() in PHP.

parseFloat()
: Parses strings as floats, like PHP's floatval().

You use isNaN() to determine if the result of an arithmetic operation was successful, because the NaN value doesn't compare to anything, including itself:

```
NaN === NaN;          // false
1 * 'two' === NaN;    // false
isNaN(1 * 'two');     // true
```

parseInt() takes an argument to parse and a second argument, which specifies how you want the string to be parsed. You can always pass 10 to make sure your input is treated as a decimal; otherwise, the interpreter would have to guess:

```
parseInt(08);        // 8
parseInt("08");      // 0
parseInt("08", 10);  // 8
```

 In strict mode, ES5 parseInt("08") now returns 8.

Let's see another example of using parseInt(). Say you want to convert CSS hexadecimal color definitions to rgb():

```
var red = '#ff0000', r, g, b;
r = red[1] + red[2]; // "ff"
g = red[3] + red[4]; // "00"
b = red[5] + red[6]; // "00"
r = parseInt(r, 16); // Parse as hexadecimal
g = parseInt(g, 16); // hex
b = parseInt(b, 16); // hex

"rgb(" + r + ", " + g + ", " + b + ")"; // "rgb(255, 0, 0)"
```

Array access to strings (e.g., red[1]) is defined in ES5 and doesn't work in old IEs.

Another example: the geeky joke that Halloween is actually Christmas because everybody knows Oct 31 = Dec 25. Using a JavaScript console, you can check if you got the joke. October = Oct = Octal = 8, December = Dec = Decimal = 10, and so:

```
parseInt(31, 8) === parseInt(25, 10); // true
```

Encoding URLs

The other four of the global functions deal with URL encodings:

encodeURIComponent() *and* decodeURIComponent()

These two functions are like PHP's urlencode() and urldecode().

encodeURI() *and* decodeURI()

These are similar to encodeURIComponent() and decodeURIComponent() but they produce valid URLs while encoding only the part that needs encoding, leaving things like http:// untouched:

```
var url = 'http://phpied.com/?search=js php';
encodeURIComponent(url); // "http%3A%2F%2Fphpied.com%2F%3Fsearch%3Djs%20php"
encodeURI(url);          // "http://phpied.com/?search=js%20php"
```

Note that encodeURI() doesn't encode "&", which may be a problem or a feature depending on what you're trying to do with query strings:

```
var qs = 'hello=world&jello=m o o n';
encodeURIComponent(qs); // "hello%3Dworld%26jello%3Dm%20o%20o%20n"
encodeURI(qs);          // "hello=world&jello=m%20o%20o%20n"
```

You may also come across the functions escape() and unescape(). These are not part of ECMAScript; they come from BOM. They work slightly differently than encodeURI() and encodeURIComponent(), and should not be used.

Built-In Constructors

Most of the built-in, ready-to-use functionality in JavaScript is implemented in its global constructor functions and two "other" global objects: either as properties and methods of the constructor functions themselves or as part of their prototype properties. The constructors can be split into four groups:

`Object()`, `Array()`, `RegExp()`, *and* `Function()`

These are rarely used to create objects, because they have shorter literal syntax versions. However, their prototypes are full of useful properties, no matter how you create the object.

`String()`, `Number()`, *and* `Boolean()`

These are also rarely used directly to create objects, because they are just wrappers around primitive types. In JavaScript, you can jump easily between the primitive type and its objectified wrapper, and you can call methods directly on the primitive.

`Date()`

Has tons of methods to work with dates.

`Error()`

Creates error objects. Error objects are simple and you can opt in for throwing your own error objects and forget all about the `Error()` constructor. `Error()` is generic, there are also more specific error constructors (e.g., `SyntaxError()`, `ReferenceError()`, etc.).

There are two more global objects worth mentioning:

`Math`

This is not a constructor (so you cannot do `var m = new Math();`), but is a global object where you can find a number of useful math-related properties and methods. For example:

```
Math.min(3, 5); // 3
Math.E; // 2.718281828459045
```

`JSON`

This is not a constructor either, but is rather an object that holds methods for encoding/decoding JSON strings. It's a new addition to ECMAScript 5, and you'll read more about it in Chapter 6.

Let's examine all these constructors in more detail.

Object

The `Object` constructor creates objects like so:

```
var o = new Object();
```

This is equivalent to the object literal notation:

```
var o = {};
```

Given that the literal is shorter, there's no reason to use the constructor directly.

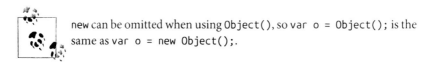

new can be omitted when using Object(), so var o = Object(); is the same as var o = new Object();.

The Object constructor also accepts an argument. Based on the argument type, Object() works as a factory and delegates the object creation to another constructor (e.g., String() or Boolean()):

```
var s = new Object('hello');
s.constructor === String; // true
```

And that is another reason to avoid calling new Object() directly. Sometimes you just don't know what type of object you'll get back.

toString()

The method toString() exists on the Object.prototype, so you can use it like so:

```
var o = {};
o.toString(); // "[object Object]"
```

Or also:

```
var o = {};
Object.prototype.toString.call(o); // "[object Object]"
```

This method gives you a string representation of the object.

The string "[object Object]" is the same for any object, so:

```
Object.prototype.toString({}) === Object.prototype.toString({a: 1}); // true
```

The method toString() is commonly used to test whether an object is an array. As it turns out, it's a little tricky to test if something is an array or not (after all, arrays *are* objects). Although it may appear a little hacky, a good and robust pattern is to use toString().

Consider the following:

```
var a = [];

var array_like = {
  length: 1,
  0: 1
};
```

If you test with:

```
if ('length' in array_like) {}
```

or

```
if (array_like.hasOwnProperty('0')) {}
```

or a similar "duck typing" pattern, you may get a false positive if it happens that the `array_like` object has the same properties. *Duck typing* means guessing the type based on some expected properties. As the saying goes, "If it walks like a duck and quacks like a duck, it must be a duck."

Another option is to use the `instanceof` operator. It works in most cases, but gets confused in IE when iframes are involved:

```
a instanceof Array;          // true
array_like instanceof Array; // false
```

Using `toString()`, you can disambiguate:

```
function isArray(a) {
  return Object.prototype.toString.call(a) === "[object Array]";
}

isArray(a);          // true
isArray(array_like); // false
```

Note the use of `toString()` as a member of `Object.prototype`, not of `Array.proto` type. This is because arrays have their own customized `toString()` that returns a string representation of the array:

```
var a = [1, 2, 'a'];
a.toString(); // "1,2,a"
```

`toString()` returns the internal class used to create an object. Here it's used to tell arrays from objects, but you can use it for more detailed introspection when `typeof` is not enough. For example:

```
typeof (/[a-z]/);              // "object"
({}).toString.call(/[a-z]/); // "[object RegExp]"

// Introspect DOM objects
({}).toString.call(document.images); // "[object HTMLCollection]"
({}).toString.call(document.querySelectorAll('*')); // "[object NodeList]"

// Tell native JSON from a "shim" implementation
// "[object JSON]" (native)
// "[object Object]" (user-land)
({}).toString.call(JSON); // "[object JSON]"
```

toLocaleString()

The method `toLocaleString()` is the same as `toString()`, only it returns the string in the current locale:

```
({}).toLocaleString(); // "[object Object]"
```

valueOf()

This method depends on the type of object. For regular objects such as arrays, regular expressions, and functions, it returns the object itself:

```
var o = {}, a = [];
o.valueOf() === o; // true
a.valueOf() === a; // true
```

For objects created by the primitive wrappers Number(), Boolean(), and String(), it returns the primitive value. For Date objects, it returns a timestamp (same as the get Time() method):

```
new Number(9).valueOf() === 9;          // true
new String("boo").valueOf() === "boo"; // true
typeof (new Date()).valueOf();          // "number"
```

hasOwnProperty()

You already know a bit about the method hasOwnProperty(). It lets you differentiate between own methods and methods that have come down the prototype chain:

```
({}).hasOwnProperty('toString'); // false
({}).constructor.prototype.hasOwnProperty('toString'); // true
```

Or another example using your own objects:

```
var papa = {name: "Papa"};
var KiddoConstructor = function () {};
KiddoConstructor.prototype = papa;

var kiddo = new KiddoConstructor();

kiddo.name;                       // "Papa"
kiddo.hasOwnProperty('name'); // false
papa.hasOwnProperty('name');  // true
```

propertyIsEnumerable()

The method propertyIsEnumerable() lets you introspect an object and see if a property will come up in a for-in loop.

For example, arrays have a length property that doesn't show up in a for-in loop:

```
[].hasOwnProperty('length');        // true
[].propertyIsEnumerable('length'); // false
```

To avoid confusion when iterating with a for-in loop, it's a common practice to check hasOwnProperty() inside the loop just to make sure you don't get any unexpected properties (e.g., properties that are added to Object.prototype):

```
var obj = {};
for (var prop in obj) {
```

```
  if (!obj.hasOwnProperty(prop)) {
    continue; // Filter out
  }

  // Real work here ...
}
```

isPrototypeOf()

As the name suggests, the method `isPrototypeOf()` helps you introspect objects:

```
Array.isPrototypeOf({});           // false
Array.prototype.isPrototypeOf({}); // false
Array.prototype.isPrototypeOf([]); // true
```

This method also follows the inheritance chain:

```
Object.prototype.isPrototypeOf([]); // true
                                    // Arrays are objects
```

constructor

As illustrated previously, `constructor` is a property that lets you figure out which constructor function was used to create the object:

```
({}).constructor === Object; // true
({}).constructor === Array;  // false
```

Since only one specific constructor was used to create the object, you cannot use the `constructor` property to look up the inheritance chain the way you'd do with `isPrototypeOf()`:

```
([]).constructor === Array;  // true
([]).constructor === Object; // false
```

This wraps up the discussion of the base `Object()` constructor. Now on to arrays.

Array

The `Array()` constructor creates arrays using the arguments passed to it as elements of the array:

```
var a = new Array(1, 2, "boom!");
a.length; // 3
a[0];     // 1
a[1];     // 2
a[2];     // "boom!"
```

Omitting new also works:

```
var a = Array(1, 2);
a.length; // 2
```

If you pass only one argument, and this argument is an integer, you'll get an array where the length equals the numeric value of the argument:

```
var a = new Array(12);
a.length; // 12
a[0];     // undefined
```

Passing a float causes an error:

```
var a = new Array(1.2); // RangeError: Invalid array length
```

Passing a string works as usual:

```
var a = new Array("12");
a.length; // 1
a[0];     // "12"
```

Instead of using new Array(), you're much better off using the array literal. It's shorter and avoids ambiguity when creating an array with one element:

```
var a = [];              // Array with no elements
var a = [1, 2, "boom"]; // Three elements
var a = [12];            // One element
```

So when translating from PHP in your mind, think that:

```
// PHP < 5.4
$a = array(1, 2);
// PHP 5.4
$a = [1, 2];

// JavaScript
var a = [1, 2];
```

Let's take a look at the properties and methods provided by Array.prototype.

length

Similar to count() in PHP, the length property gives you the number of elements:

```
[1, 2, 3, 4].length; // 4
```

But be aware that length is mutable:

```
var a = [1, 2, 3, 4];
a.length; // 4
a.length = 100;
a.length; // 100
```

In this case, elements a[4] through a[99] don't exist, and you'll get undefined if you ask for their values, for example, in a loop from 0 to a.length.

Consider the following:

```
var a = [1, 2, 3, 4];
a.length = 100;
```

```
a[10];     // undefined
99 in a; // false
```

Somewhat similar is this example:

```
var a = [1, 2, 3, 4];
a[99] = undefined;
a.length; // 100
```

The difference is that here the element a[99] exists because you've created it, even if it has the undefined value. All other elements a[4] through a[98] do not exist:

```
var a = [1, 2, 3, 4];
a[99] = undefined;
99 in a;  // true
98 in a;  // false
a.length; // 100
```

Note the difference with PHP. Implementing the preceding code in PHP gives you five elements and doesn't change the value that count($a) returns:

```
// PHP
$a = array(1, 2, 3, 4);
$a[99] = null;
echo count($a); // 5
```

push()

Just like array_push() in PHP, Array.prototype.push() appends an element to the end of the array:

```
// PHP
$a = array(1, 2);
array_push($a, 3, 4);

// JavaScript
var a = [1, 2];
a.push(3, 4);
a.toString(); // "1,2,3,4"
```

Array.prototype.push() returns the length of the updated array:

```
[1, 2].push("a", "b"); // 4
```

pop()

The opposite of push() is pop(). It removes the last element from the array and returns it:

```
// PHP
$a = array(1, 2, 3);
$what = array_pop($a);
echo count($a); // 2
echo $what;     // 3
```

```
// JavaScript
var a = [1, 2, 3];
var what = a.pop();
a.toString(); // "1,2"
what; // 3
```

unshift()

`Array.prototype.unshift()` is like `Array.prototype.push()` but adds the new element to the beginning of the array. It also returns the new length. The PHP equivalent is `array_unshift()`:

```
// PHP
$a = array(1, 2);
$count = array_unshift($a, 3, 4);
print_r($a); // Array ( [0] => 3 [1] => 4 [2] => 1 [3] => 2 )
echo $count; // 4

// JavaScript
var a = [1, 2];
var count = a.unshift(3, 4);
a.toString(); // "3,4,1,2"
count;         // 4
```

shift()

`shift()` is the opposite of `unshift()`. It removes the first element of the array and returns it. It's JavaScript's equivalent of PHP's `array_shift()`:

```
// PHP
$a = array(1, 2, 3);
$first = array_shift($a);
print_r($a); // Array ( [0] => 2 [1] => 3 )
echo $first; // 1

// JavaScript
var a = [1, 2, 3];
var first = a.shift();
a.toString(); // "2,3"
first;         // 1
```

concat()

`Array.prototype.concat()` is similar to PHP's `array_merge()`. It creates a new array by appending the elements of one array to the end of another. Both input arrays remain unchanged:

```
var a = [1, 2, 3];
var b = ['one', 'two', 'three'];
var c = a.concat(b);

a.toString(); // "1,2,3"
```

```
b.toString(); // "one,two,three"
c.toString(); // "1,2,3,one,two,three"
```

You can pass multiple arguments to `concat()`. If they are not arrays, they are treated as if they were arrays with a single value:

```
var c = a.concat(b, "boo", ["boom", "vroom"], "oink");
c.toString(); // "1,2,3,one,two,three,boo,boom,vroom,oink"
```

sort()

In PHP, there are many functions you can use to sort arrays, but in JavaScript, there's only one: `Array.prototype.sort()`. It takes a function callback that allows you to implement your custom sorting:

```
var a = ["Paul", "John", "Ringo", "George"];
a.sort().toString(); // "George,John,Paul,Ringo"
```

A common task that `sort()` doesn't address out of the box is sorting numbers:

```
var nums = [1, 9, 10, 2, 11];
nums.sort().toString(); // "1,10,11,2,9"
```

Probably not what you expected: the numbers were sorted as strings. As if you used SORT_STRING in PHP's `sort()`:

```
// PHP
$nums = array(1, 9, 10, 2, 11);
sort($nums, SORT_STRING);
print_r($nums); // Array ( [0] => 1 [1] => 10 [2] => 11 [3] => 2 [4] => 9 )
```

If you need the equivalent of SORT_NUMERIC, you need to implement your callback function in JavaScript:

```
var nums = [1, 9, 10, 2, 11];
nums.sort(function (a, b) {
  return a - b;
});
nums.toString(); // "1,2,9,10,11"
```

As you can see, the callback works like a callback you'd pass to `usort()` in PHP. It returns:

- 0 if the two elements passed to it are equal
- A positive number if the first argument is considered larger than the second
- A negative number if the first argument is considered smaller than the second

How about shuffling, or randomizing, an array? PHP has `array_shuffle()`, but there's no equivalent in JavaScript. Since randomizing can be thought of as sorting but in random order, it means you can provide a callback that returns a random result. `Math.ran dom()` returns a random number between 0 and 1, but you need negative numbers, too, so you can just subtract the random number from 0.5 to have an equal probability of getting a positive or a negative result:

```
var nums = [1, 2, 9, 10, 11];
nums.sort(function (a, b) {
  return 0.5 - Math.random();
});
nums.toString(); // "11,1,9,2,10"
```

slice()

`Array.prototype.slice()` returns a new array created by cutting a piece of the original array between a given start and end index:

```
var a = ['one', 'and', 'two', 'and', 'three', 'and', 'four'];
var b = a.slice(2, 5);
b.toString(); // "two,and,three"
```

 `Array.prototype.slice()` is similar to PHP's `array_slice()` but not exactly equivalent because PHP's `array_slice()` takes a start index and a length, not an end index.

If you omit the second argument when calling `slice()`, it defaults to the `length`:

```
var a = ['one', 'and', 'two', 'and', 'three', 'and', 'four'];
var b = a.slice(2);
b.toString(); // "two,and,three,and,four"
```

If you pass a negative index `i`, the value of this argument becomes `a.length + i`. So, if you need the last three elements, you can do the following:

```
var a = ['one', 'and', 'two', 'and', 'three', 'and', 'four'];
a.slice(-3).toString(); // "three,and,four"
```

This is because the `a.length` is 7, and so the argument becomes 7 + (-3).

So it's equivalent to:

```
var a = ['one', 'and', 'two', 'and', 'three', 'and', 'four'];
a.slice(4).toString(); // "three,and,four"
```

splice()

`Array.prototype.splice()` is a powerful method for working with arrays. It's a good idea to play around with it.

The `splice()` method can add and remove elements at the same time. It removes elements by given start index and length. Then, in the "vacuum" created by the missing elements, you can insert other ones.

It's similar to PHP's `array_splice()`.

Note the difference with `Array.prototype.slice()`, however. `splice()` takes a start index and a length (number of elements) to remove, while `slice()` takes start and end index:

```
// PHP
$input = array("red", "green", "blue", "yellow", "purple");
$slice = array_splice($input, 2, 2, "orange");
print_r($input); // "red", "green", "orange", "purple"
print_r($slice); // "blue", "yellow"

// JavaScript
var input = ["red", "green", "blue", "yellow", "purple"];
var slice = input.splice(2, 2, "orange");
input.toString(); // "red,green,orange,purple"
slice.toString(); // "blue,yellow"
```

You can add as many new elements to replace the sliced out ones and, if they are not arrays, they'll be treated as arrays with one element:

```
var input = ["red", "green", "blue", "yellow", "purple"];
input.splice(2, 2, "orange", ["black", "white"], "grey");
input.toString(); // "red,green,orange,black,white,grey,purple"
```

reverse()

As the name suggests, `Array.prototype.reverse()` reverses the order of the array elements (the last element becomes the first, etc.), similar to PHP's `array_reverse()`:

```
[1, 2, 3].reverse().toString(); // "3,2,1"
```

join()

`Array.prototype.join()` is like PHP's `implode()`. It returns a string made of the elements of the array, delimited by a string. The default delimiter is comma:

```
[5, 4, 3].join(' > '); // "5 > 4 > 3"
[5, 4, 3].join();      // "5,4,3"
                       // same as toString()
[5, 4, 3].join('');    // "543"
```

In PHP, the opposite of `implode()` is explode(), and in JavaScript, the opposite of `Array.prototype.join()` is `String.prototype.split()`, which you'll see in a bit.

At this point, you're done with arrays. Let's consider regular expressions next.

RegExp

The `RegExp` constructor creates regular expression objects. It can be used with and without new. It also has an alternative syntax that uses a regular expression literal:

```
var re = new RegExp('[a-z]');  // Constructor
var re = RegExp('[a-z]');      // Constructor without `new`
var re = /[a-z]/;              // Literal
```

As you see, the literal is shorter and easier. You only need to use the constructor when creating the regex pattern on the fly by concatenating strings.

 In ES3, regular expression objects defined with the literal notation are created only once during the parsing stage:

```
function gimme() {
  return /a-z/;
}

var a = gimme();
var b = gimme();
a === b; // false, but true in ES3
```

You can also specify any of the three regex modifiers:

- global (using g)—match all occurrences, not just the first
- multiline (using m)
- ignoreCase (i)

You can set them in any order. They are all false by default:

```
var re = new RegExp('[a-z]', 'gmi');
var re = /[a-z]/ig;

// test
re.ignoreCase; // true
re.multiline;  // false
```

test() and properties

After you've created the regex object, you can use exec() and test() to match strings. exec() returns matches, while test() only returns true/false if at least one match was found:

```
re.exec("somestring"); // Returns matches
re.test("somestring"); // Returns true|false
```

Additional properties of the regex object are as follows:

```
re.lastIndex;  // The index of the last match
re.source;     // The regex pattern as a string (e.g., "[a-z]")
re.global;     // Whether the `g` flag was set
re.multiline;  // Whether the `m` flag was set
re.ignoreCase; // Whether the `i` flag was set
```

exec()

When you use `re.exec()`, the return value is an array of matches plus two more properties: `input` and `index`, which are respectively the input string to be matched and the index of the match.

Let's see an example in more detail:

```
var re = /([dn])(o+)/;
var result = re.exec("doodle noodle");
result.join(', '); // "doo, d, oo"
```

As you can see, `result` is an array. It contains the full match (doo) and the matches of the grouping () within the regex pattern. You can also see that the `result` array has the extra properties `input` and `index`:

```
result.input; // "doodle noodle"
result.index; // 0
```

 Arrays are objects, so it's OK for them to have additional properties besides the numeric ones 0, 1, 2…

If you call `re.exec()` again, you'll get the exact same result. But the regex pattern is supposed to also match "noo." To get all matches, you need the g modifier:

```
var re = /([dn])(o+)/g;
```

Then you call `exec()` in a loop and get the next match. With every match, the property `re.lastIndex` gets updated with the index character where the match ends. When `re.exec()` returns `null` (which also causes `re.lastIndex` to become 0 again), that's your signal that there are no more matches:

```
var re = /([dn])(o+)/g;
var str = "doodle noodle";

re.lastIndex; // 0

re.exec(str); // ["doo", "d", "oo"]
re.lastIndex; // 3

re.exec(str); // ["noo", "n", "oo"]
re.lastIndex; // 10

re.exec(str); // null
re.lastIndex; // 0
```

The same example as a loop:

```
var re = /([dn])(o+)/g;
var str = "doodle noodle";
var match;

while (match = re.exec(str)) {
  // Do something with `match` or `re.lastIndex`
  console.log(match);
  console.log(re.lastIndex);
}
```

Function

You can use the Function constructor to create function objects:

```
var f = new Function('a', 'b', 'return a + b');
f(4, 5); // 9
```

As you can see, this way of creating functions is cumbersome and smells of eval(), so it should be avoided as much as possible. Although Function() can be used wisely for some metaprogramming tasks, for most common problems, JavaScript is dynamic enough so you rarely need to write code as a string.

One use of Function() is to replace eval() because Function() creates a local scope and doesn't bleed variables after the evaluation. Consider:

```
var code = "var tmp = 1; console.log(tmp);";
Function(code)(); // Logs 1
typeof tmp;       // undefined

eval(code); // Logs 1
typeof tmp; // "number"
```

As you can see, you can omit new with Function, too.

Function() not only doesn't bleed variables into the global space, but it also has nothing in its scope chain except the global scope:

```
// Global namespace
var globe = "round";

(function () {
  var globe = "flat";

  (new Function("return globe;"))(); // "round"

  eval("return globe;"); // "flat"
}());
```

Function properties

You already know about all properties and methods of the function object:

---

length
> Expected number of arguments

name
> Name of the function, not part of the ECMAScript standard

call()
> Executes a function passing individual arguments

apply()
> Executes a function passing all arguments as an array

An example:

```
// Define a function
function sum() {
  var res = 0;
  for (var i = 0; i < arguments.length; i++) {
    res += arguments[i];
  }
  return res;
}

// Test properties
sum.length; // 0
sum.name;   // "sum"

// Test methods
sum.call(null, 1, 2, 3);      // 6
sum.apply(null, [2, 2, 2, 2]); // 8
```

The first argument passed to call() and apply() is the object to be assigned to this inside the body of the function. When you don't care about this, you pass null.

String

String() used as a constructor with new creates string objects. String() used as a function without new casts the argument to a primitive string. String objects are different from string primitives, but you can access properties and methods of a primitive string (and boolean and number) as if it were an object. There's not much reason to use the new String() constructor directly:

```
// Constructor, creates string objects
var s = new String("hello");
typeof s; // "object"

// Without `new` it creates string primitives
var s = String("hello");
typeof s; // "string"

// Best used as a primitive
```

```
var s = "hello";
typeof s; // "string"

// You can call methods and properties on primitives too
s.length;    // 5
"hi".length; // 2

// You can't add properties to primitives though
var sp = "primitive";
sp.likes_caves = true;
sp.length;        // 9
sp.likes_caves; // undefined
```

Table 5-1 lists the basic properties and methods of String.prototype by comparing them with PHP functions.

Table 5-1. Methods of String.prototype compared to PHP's functions

JavaScript	PHP	Result
var s = "JavaScript";	$s = "JavaScript";	
s.length;	echo strlen($s);	10
s.indexOf("a");	echo strpos($s, 'a');	1
s.lastIndexOf("a");	echo strrpos($s, 'a');	3
s.charAt(0);	echo $s[0];	"J"
s.charCodeAt(0);	echo ord($s[0]);	74
s.toLowerCase();	echo strtolower($s);	"javascript"
s.toLocaleLowerCase();		
s.toUpperCase();	echo strtoupper($s);	"JAVASCRIPT"
s.toLocaleUpperCase();		
s.concat(" rulz", "!");	echo $s . " rulz" . "!";	"JavaScript rulz!"

These were the simplest methods; now let's discuss the others in some more detail.

substring()

There are three methods that allow you to extract a piece of a string:

```
var s = "JavaScript";
s.slice(4, 7);     // "Scr"
s.substring(4, 7); // "Scr"
s.substr(4, 3);    // "Scr", nonstandard
```

The first two, slice() and substring(), are similar to PHP's substr(), only they take a start and end index as opposed to start index and length. The nonstandard substr() in JavaScript takes start and length, so it's just like substr() in PHP.

localeCompare()

`String.prototype.localeCompare()` is like PHP's `strcmp()`. It allows you to compare strings based on how they would be sorted:

```
"JavaScript".localeCompare("Java") > 0; // true
```

It returns 0 if the two strings are equal, a positive integer if the argument is smaller (meaning it will be sorted before the original string), and a negative integer otherwise. The exact value of the integer varies between JavaScript interpreters.

```
"JavaScript".localeCompare("JavaScripz") < 0; // true
```

split()

`String.prototype.split()` is similar to PHP's `explode()`. It splits the string into an array based on a delimiter string:

```
"a,b,c".split(','); // ["a", "b", "c"]
```

It also allows the delimiter to be a regular expression:

```
var s = "JavaScript";
s.split(/a/); // ["J", "v", "Script"]
```

A regular expression can help you parse sloppily spaced CSV (comma-separated values) data. For example:

```
"a,   b  , c".split(/\s*,\s*/); // ["a", "b", "c"]
```

search()

As the name suggests, `String.prototype.search()` finds an occurrence of a string within a string. It's similar in purpose to PHP's `strstr()`, but the implementation is closer to PHP's `strpos()`:

```
var s = "JavaScript";
s.search(/ava/);  // 1
s.search("Java"); // 0
```

Two things to point out here:

- You can search using either a regular expression or a string.

- Be careful with 0 results—this is a match at index 0. If a match is not found, you'll get -1:

```
// BAD
if (!s.search('Java')) {
  // false negative, this is executed
  alert('not found!');
}
```

```
// better
if (s.search('Java') === -1) {
  alert('not found!');
}
```

replace()

PHP has `str_replace()` and JavaScript has `String.prototype.replace()` to search and replace contents of strings. They work differently though.

First of all, `replace()` takes a regular expression to search for:

```
"JavaScript".replace(/a/g, "@"); // "J@v@Script"
```

If you only pass a string, its content is used as a pattern of a regular expression. But because in this case you cannot set the g modifier of the regular expression pattern, only the first occurrence is replaced:

```
"JavaScript".replace("a", "@"); // "J@vaScript"
```

This is a common source of errors. Always using a regular expression "needle" to search for is a good habit, even if you only mean to replace the first occurrence.

Second, `replace()` doesn't take arrays as inputs as PHP does, so you'll have to chain method calls:

```
// PHP
$s = "JavaScript";
$s = str_replace(array("a", "S"), array("@", "$"), $s);
echo $s; // "J@v@$cript"

// JavaScript
var s = "JavaScript";
s = s.replace(/a/g, "@").replace(/s/gi, '$');
s; // "J@v@$cript"
```

And lastly, `replace()` can take a callback function instead of a literal string as a replacement. The match, the index of the match, and the original input string are passed as arguments to the callback function, and the callback can do interesting and conditional replacements based on the match.

The following example substitutes lowercase letters with HTML entity codes:

```
var ents = "JavaScript".replace(/[a-z]/g, function (match, index, input) {
  // `match` is a, then v, then a, and so on
  // `index` is the index of the match: 1, 2, 3, 5, 6...
  // `input` is "JavaScript"
  return "&#".concat(match.charCodeAt(0), ";");
});
```

The result is:

```
ents; // "J&#97;&#118;&#97;S&#99;&#114;&#105;&#112;&#116;"
```

match()

`String.prototype.match()` matches a regular expression pattern, similar to PHP's `preg_match()` and `preg_match_all()`:

```
// PHP
$s = "JavaScript";
preg_match("/[A-Z]/", $s, $matches);
preg_match_all("/[A-Z]/", $s, $matches_all);
print_r($matches);      // matches J
print_r($matches_all); // matches J and S

// JavaScript
var s = "JavaScript";
s.match(/[A-Z]/);  // ["J"]
s.match(/[A-Z]/g); // ["J", "S"]
```

When the regular expression doesn't use the global **g** modifier, the method works the same as the exec() method of the regular expression objects:

```
"string".match(/[a-z]/); // ["s"]
/[a-z]/.exec("string");  // ["s"]
```

When no match is found, you get `null` back, not an empty array:

```
"string".match(/[0-9]/); // null
/[0-9]/.exec("string");  // null
```

Number

The `Number()` constructor wraps the primitive number type. It can be used to convert strings to numbers:

```
Number("1.1"); // 1.1
```

It's less forgiving than `parseInt()` or `parseFloat()`:

```
Number("3,14");        // NaN
parseInt("3,14", 10);  // 3
parseFloat("3,14", 10); // 3
```

As with `String()`, new `Number()` creates number objects, while `Number()` without new returns primitive numbers:

```
typeof Number("1.1");     // "number"
typeof new Number("1.1"); // "object"
```

There are few constants defined as properties of the `Number()` function:

```
Number.MAX_VALUE;        // 1.7976931348623157e+308
Number.MIN_VALUE;        // 5e-324
Number.POSITIVE_INFINITY; // Infinity
Number.NEGATIVE_INFINITY; // -Infinity
Number.NaN;              // NaN
```

And finally, there are three methods of `Number.prototype`:

```
Number(123).toFixed(2);          // "123.00"
(1000000000000).toExponential(); // "1e+12"
(1000000000000).toPrecision(3);  // "1.00e+12"
```

As you can see, methods of the primitive numbers can be called as if they were objects. Wrap them in parentheses (grouping operator) when you need to work with literal numbers.

Boolean

`Boolean()` is the most useless of the three primitive wrapper constructors. It has no additional properties or methods. It can also be confusing—new `Boolean()` returns an object, and all objects are truthy:

```
!!new Boolean(true);  // true
!!new Boolean(false); // true
```

Math

`Math` is not a constructor but an object (a property of the global object) that's used as a namespace to contain useful constants and methods.

Constants are the following:

```
Math.E;       // 2.718281828459045
Math.LN2;     // 0.6931471805599453
Math.LN10;    // 2.302585092994046
Math.LOG2E;   // 1.4426950408889634
Math.LOG10E;  // 0.4342944819032518
Math.PI;      // 3.141592653589793
Math.SQRT1_2; // 0.7071067811865476
Math.SQRT2;   // 1.4142135623730951
```

And the methods are pretty self-explanatory:

```
// Rounding
Math.round(5.6); // 6
Math.floor(5.6); // 5
Math.ceil(5.1);  // 6

// Geometry
Math.sin(); Math.cos(); Math.tan();
Math.asin(); Math.acos(); Math.atan(); Math.atan2();

// min/max
Math.max(1, 2, 3, -1); // 3
Math.min(1, 2, 3, -1); // -1

// Powers and roots
Math.sqrt(49);  // 7
```

```
Math.pow(7, 2); // 49

// Random number between 0 and 1
Math.random(); // 0.17569443793036044

// log/exp
Math.exp();
Math.log();
```

Error

You can throw your own errors with new Error() or any of the other error constructors. These objects have only two standard cross-browser properties that you can rely on: name and message.

The name property contains the name of the constructor (as a string)—for example, "Error", "ReferenceError", and so on.

You might as well forget all about the built-in error constructors and throw your own objects:

```
if (2 + 2 > 4) {
  throw {
    name: "CrazyError",
    message: "It's the end of the world as we know it"
  };
}
```

For completeness, here are the other error constructors:

- EvalError

- RangeError

- ReferenceError

- SyntaxError

- TypeError

- URIError

Date

Date() creates date objects:

```
var d = new Date(2013, 11, 31); // December 31, 2013
```

You can also specify the optional hour, minute, second, and millisecond:

```
new Date(2013, 11, 31, 23, 59, 59, 999); // One millisecond before 2014
```

Alternatively, you can create a date object from a timestamp or a string:

```
new Date(0); // Dec 31, 1969
new Date("December 31, 1969");
```

Passing a string is similar in purpose to PHP's strtotime(), although not as powerful.

Two methods exist as properties of the Date() constructor:

- parse()
- UTC()

parse() is the same as passing a string to new Date() only it returns a timestamp, not an object. Date.UTC() is like the Date() constructor with the long list of arguments (year, month, and optionally day, hour, minute, second, millisecond), only UTC() returns a timestamp in universal time, as opposed to an object in local time.

Then there are many methods on the Date.prototype. They are self-explanatory, so there's no point of discussing them in detail. The full list is as follows:

```
var d = new Date(0); // Dec 31, 1969, local

// Local on my computer time is PST,
// meaning 8 hours (480 minutes) behind UTC
d.getTimezoneOffset(); // 480

// get/set date
d.setYear(2020); // 1609459200000
d.getYear();       // 120, year counted from 1900

d.setFullYear(2020);    // 1609459200000
d.setUTCFullYear(2020); // 1577836800000
d.getFullYear();        // 2019, local time
d.getUTCFullYear();     // 2020

d.setMonth(11);    // 1577836800000
d.setUTCMonth(11); // 1606780800000
d.getMonth();      // 10 , November, because it's local
d.getUTCMonth();   // 11, December, as set

d.setDate(31);    // 1606867200000
d.setUTCDate(31); // 1609372800000
d.getDate();      // 30, local
d.getUTCDate();   // 31

// At this point, the date has become
// "Wed Dec 30 2020" local
// "Thu, 31 Dec 2020" UTC

d.getDay();    // 3, because 0: Sunday, 1: Monday... 3: Wednesday
d.getUTCDay(); // 4, Thursday
```

```
d.setHours(0);     // 1609315200000
d.setUTCHours(0); // 1609286400000
d.getHours();      // 16, because 24 - 8 = 16
d.getUTCHours();   // 0

d.setMinutes(30);     // 1609288200000
d.setUTCMinutes(30); // 1609288200000
d.getMinutes();       // 30
d.getUTCMinutes();    // 30

d.setSeconds(30);     // 1609288230000
d.setUTCSeconds(30); // 1609288230000
d.getSeconds();       // 30
d.getUTCSeconds();    // 30

// 1000 ms is 1 second, so setting to 1000 moves the
// date 1 second ahead
d.setMilliseconds(1000);     // 1609288231000
d.setUTCMilliseconds(1000); // 1609288232000
d.getMilliseconds(0);
d.getUTCMilliseconds(0);

d.setTime(0); // Unix timestamp
d.getTime();  // 0

// Miscellaneous toString variations
d.toString();       // "Wed Dec 31 1969 16:00:00 GMT-0800 (PST)"
d.toLocaleString(); // "Wed Dec 31 1969 16:00:00 GMT-0800 (PST)"
d.toUTCString();    // "Thu, 01 Jan 1970 00:00:00 GMT"
d.toGMTString();    // "Thu, 01 Jan 1970 00:00:00 GMT"

d.toDateString();       // "Wed Dec 31 1969"
d.toLocaleDateString(); // "Wednesday, December 31, 1969"

d.toTimeString();       // "16:00:00 GMT-0800 (PST)"
d.toLocaleTimeString(); // "16:00:00"
```

Casting a date object to a number (e.g., using Number() or an arithmetic operation) gives you the Unix timestamp, like just like getTime():

```
var d = new Date();
Number(d) === d.getTime(); // true

new Date().getTime() === +new Date(); // true
```

Constructors Review

At this point, you've seen of JavaScript's constructors, as well as their properties and the properties of their prototypes. It doesn't make sense to use most of them directly as constructors because there are shorter literal versions that are as good or better. Here's a quick cheat sheet:

`Object()`
It's better to use the object literal {} instead.

`Array()`
Use literal [ ] instead.

`RegExp()`
Use literal `/[a-z]/` when the pattern is static.

`Function()`
Use a function declaration or a function expression instead.

`String()`
Just define a regular primitive `"string"` and use this constructor only for type casting.

`Number()`
Use only for type casting; otherwise, numbers are better defined as primitives.

`Boolean()`
Useless; just use `true` and `false` literally.

`Error()`
Just throw your own errors (e.g., `SyntaxError()`, etc.).

`Date()`
The only constructor you can't get without.

`Math`
Not a constructor, but a useful namespace for math constants and static methods.

`JSON`
Also not a constructor, but a global object you'll see again in Chapter 6.

ECMAScript 5

This book has mostly talked about ECMAScript 3 because it's the most widely distributed version of the language. However, the latest standard is ECMAScript 5.1 (version 4 was a dead-end branch that was eventually scrapped). Most modern browsers support ES5. You should know about what's new in ES5 even if you currently have to support legacy browsers.

The three main areas of updates are:

- Introduction of strict mode
- Object and property attributes
- Some new APIs

Strict Mode

Strict mode is not backward compatible, and is therefore an opt-in feature. Once per function or once per program you can opt into strict mode by using:

```
"use strict";
```

Since this is just a string statement, old browsers won't complain and will simply ignore it. But an engine that understands strict mode will treat your code more strictly, disallowing some JavaScript features and constructs which, over the years, have proven to be more trouble than they're worth. This book doesn't teach any of these shady practices, so there's nothing for you to unlearn.

Examples of features that trigger an error in strict mode are:

- The use of the with statement
- Use of undeclared variables

- Use of `arguments.callee` or `arguments.caller`
- Attempts to assign to read-only properties (e.g., `window.Infinity = 0;`)
- Attempts to delete nonconfigurable properties (you will see what *configurable* means in a bit)
- Object literals with duplicate properties
- Function parameters with duplicate names (because, surprisingly, `function (a, a, a) {}` is OK in ES3)

Here's a simple example that illustrates how strict and nonstrict modes differ:

```
// Nonstrict
var obj = (function () {
  return {a: 1, a: 2};
})();

obj; // {a: 2}
// Strict
var obj = (function () {
  "use strict";
  return {a: 1, a: 2};
})(); // SyntaxError: duplicate property
```

Property Attributes

The second area of changes in ES5 is the introduction of property attributes. In fact, these attributes have always been around, only they were not available to the programmer to tweak.

A property can have a `value` attribute as well as three boolean attributes, which define whether the property is:

- Enumerable
- Writable
- Configurable

You can define the attributes of a property in special objects called *descriptors*. Here's an example:

```
var stealth_descriptor = {
  value: "can't touch this",
  enumerable: false, // Won't show up in for-in loops
  writable: false,   // Can't change my value
  configurable: false // Can't delete me or change my attributes
};
```

Nonconfigurable properties can only have their `writable` attribute set to nonwritable.

Property descriptors give you more control over the mutability of the property. They let you, for example, create nondeletable properties with constant values. While many of the ES5 APIs can be implemented in ES3, property descriptors are something that cannot. In ES3, all the properties you create are mutable.

You'll see more details and examples of using property descriptors in the next section.

New Object APIs

Let's take a look at the new APIs that let you play with property attributes, namely:

- `Object.create()`
- `Object.defineProperty()`
- `Object.defineProperties()`
- `Object.getOwnPropertyDescriptor()`

Object.create()

This method can be used to create a new object and at the same time:

- Define the inheritance
- Define the properties of the object
- Define the attributes of the properties

Consider the following snippet:

```
var human = {name: "John"};
var programmer = Object.create(
  human,
  {
    secret: stealth_descriptor,
    skill: {value: "Code ninja"}
  }
);
```

The `programmer` object inherits from the `human` object by way of `__proto__`, so it has (but does not own) a `name` property:

```
programmer.name; // "John"
programmer.hasOwnProperty('name'); // false
programmer.__proto__.hasOwnProperty('name'); // true
```

The other two properties are own properties:

```
programmer.hasOwnProperty('secret'); // true
programmer.hasOwnProperty('skill');  // true
```

A full descriptor was used for the secret property: the stealth_descriptor which sets the value, as well as the three attributes.

The skill property only defines a value. This means that all the attributes are set to their default values, which are all false.

If you simply set a property without a descriptor, all attributes are true, as the case is with ES3:

```
programmer.likes = ['pizza', 'beer', 'coffee'];
```

 Object.create() is similar to begetObject() (discussed in "Inheritance" on page 66) plus the addition of the descriptors.

Earlier in this book, it was explained that "empty" objects (e.g., var o = {};) are not really empty, because they inherit methods such as toString() from Object.proto type. Well, in ES5, you can create truly empty objects using:

```
var o = Object.create(null); // Inherit nothing
typeof o.toString;           // "undefined"
```

Object.getOwnPropertyDescriptor()

The getOwnPropertyDescriptor() method lets you examine the descriptor objects:

```
Object.getOwnPropertyDescriptor(programmer, 'secret').configurable; // false
Object.getOwnPropertyDescriptor(programmer, 'likes').configurable;  // true
```

Object.defineProperty() and Object.defineProperties()

The two methods Object.defineProperty() and Object.defineProperties() allow you to define properties with a descriptor at a later time, after the object was created:

```
Object.defineProperty(programmer, 'hello', stealth_descriptor);

Object.defineProperties(programmer, {
  goodbye: stealth_descriptor,
  bye: stealth_descriptor
});
```

Restricting Object Mutations

In ES3, all objects are mutable, with a few exceptions found in the built-in objects. Sometimes this is not a good idea because users of your objects can change them beyond repair. In ES5, you can restrict access to your objects. For example, you can make selected properties read-only by setting their `writable` attribute to `false`.

But you can restrict access to the whole object by:

- Preventing extensions (i.e., don't allow new properties)
- "Sealing" an object, which means making all properties nonconfigurable (cannot delete them) on top of making the object nonextensible
- "Freezing" an object, which is like sealing but with the additional step of setting all properties to nonwritable

Consider this regular object:

```
var pizza = {
  tomatoes: true,
  cheese: true
};
```

You can always add more properties:

```
pizza.pepperoni = 'lots';
```

You can change and delete properties, because they are all configurable and writable:

```
pizza.cheese = 'mozzarella';
delete pizza.pepperoni; // true
```

However, if you prevent extensions, you'll no longer be able to add properties. You can check for extensibility with `Object.isExtensible()` and disallow extensions (irreversibly) with `Object.preventExtensions()`:

```
Object.isExtensible(pizza);       // true
Object.preventExtensions(pizza); // Returns the `pizza` object
Object.isExtensible(pizza);       // false

pizza.broccoli = 'eww'; // Error, cannot add properties anymore
typeof pizza.broccoli;  // "undefined"
```

Additionally, you can prevent deletions with `seal()`:

```
Object.isSealed(pizza); // false
Object.seal(pizza);     // Returns the `pizza` object
Object.isSealed(pizza); // true

delete pizza.cheese; // Error, can't delete
pizza.cheese;        // "mozzarella"
```

You can still change a property value though:

```
pizza.cheese = 'ricotta';
```

But once you `freeze()` an object, that's it, all properties become nonwritable:

```
Object.isFrozen(pizza); // false
Object.freeze(pizza);   // Returns the `pizza` object
Object.isFrozen(pizza); // true

pizza.cheese = "gorgonzola"; // Error, `cheese` is read-only
pizza.cheese;                // "ricotta"
```

So, in review:

- `freeze()` does what `seal()` does plus sets the `writable` attribute to `false` for all properties.
- `seal()` does what `preventExtensions()` does plus sets the `configurable` attribute to `false` for all properties.
- `preventExtensions()` doesn't set any attributes, but it doesn't let you add more properties afterward.
- None of these actions can be turned back on (i.e., there's no `unfreeze()`, `defrost()`, `allowExtensions()`, etc.).

Looping Alternatives

In ES3, if you want to get a list of all properties (like `array_keys()` in PHP), then you have to do a `for-in` loop. In ES5, you can use `Object.keys()` or `Object.getOwnPropertyNames()`. The `keys()` method gives you all enumerable properties (those that will show up in a `for-in` loop), while `getOwnPropertyNames()` returns all own properties, enumerable or not.

Both methods are the same if you don't use descriptors to set the `enumerable` attributes:

```
var pizza = {tomatoes: true, cheese: true};
Object.keys(pizza);                 // ["tomatoes", "cheese"]
Object.getOwnPropertyNames(pizza); // ["tomatoes", "cheese"]
```

Both methods work with own properties only, they will not return anything inherited from the prototype. Let's create an object `pizza_v20` that inherits `pizza` and adds some new properties:

```
var pizza_v20 = Object.create(pizza, {
  salami: {value: "lots", enumerable: true},
  sauce: {value: "secret"}
});
```

`keys()` will not return `sauce` because it's not enumerable, but `getOwnProperty Names()` will return all properties:

```
Object.keys(pizza_v20);             // ["salami"]
Object.getOwnPropertyNames(pizza_v20); // ["sauce", "salami"]
```

Both don't return any of the pizza properties, because those properties are inherited:

```
pizza_v20.cheese;              // true
pizza_v20.__proto__ === pizza; // true
```

Object.getPrototypeOf()

Wrapping up the novelties in Object() in ES5, let's take a look at the getPrototy peOf() method. In ES3, you can only inspect with isPrototypeOf(), in which case you need to suspect an object and ask if that is indeed the prototype.

In ES5, you can directly ask, "Who is your prototype?"

```
Object.getPrototypeOf(pizza_v20) === pizza; // true
```

As you can see, this is the same as using __proto__, but remember that __proto__ is not standard (and doesn't exist in IE). ES5 admits there's a need for at least a readable version of __proto__ and introduces getPrototypeOf() as a replacement (a writable version is still a topic for heated debate).

Array Additions

In ES5, there are quite a few methods added to Array.prototype as well as one added to the Array constructor.

Array.isArray()

Array.isArray() gives you a nonhacky way to distinguish between arrays and objects (remember arrays *are* objects) in JavaScript.

If you want to *shim* the method and use it in ES3 as well, you can use the Object.pro totype.toString() trick, as illustrated previously in this book:

```
if (!Array.isArray) {
  Array.isArray = function (candidate) {
    return Object.prototype.toString.call(candidate) === '[object Array]';
  };
}

Array.isArray([]); // true
```

This method is the equivalent of is_array() in PHP.

indexOf() and lastIndexOf()

The two new methods `Array.prototype.indexOf()` and `Array.prototype.lastIn` `dexOf()` offer more ways to search in an array.

`Array.prototype.indexOf()` returns the index of the first occurrence of an element:

```
var a = ['one', 'and', 'two', 'and', 'three', 'and', 'four'];
a.indexOf('three'); // 4
```

This is close to PHP's `array_search()`.

While `Array.prototype.indexOf()` returns the first occurrence, `Array.proto` `type.lastIndexOf()` returns the last:

```
var a = ['one', 'and', 'two', 'and', 'three', 'and', 'four'];
a.indexOf("and");      // 1
a.lastIndexOf("and"); // 5
```

The search for elements uses strict comparison to find matches:

```
[1, 2, 100, "100"].indexOf("100"); // 3
[1, 2, 100, "100"].indexOf(100);    // 2
```

You can also specify start position in `indexOf()` or end position in `lastIndexOf()` to begin the search:

```
var arr = [100, 1, 2, 100];

arr.indexOf(100);        // 0
arr.indexOf(100, 2);     // 3

arr.lastIndexOf(100);    // 3
arr.lastIndexOf(100, 2); // 0
```

Walking the Array Elements

ES5 adds `Array.prototype.forEach()`, which allows you to loop over all array elements without a loop construct. It takes a callback function in which you can do an operation with each element or with the whole array.

Here's a quick example that logs the arguments passed to the callback function:

```
["a", "b", "c"].forEach(function () {
  console.log(arguments);
});
```

The result in the console will be:

```
["a", 0, Array[3]]
["b", 1, Array[3]]
["c", 2, Array[3]]
```

As you see, the format is:

```
[the element, its index, the whole array]
```

Filtering

ES5 adds `Array.prototype.filter()`, which, just like PHP's `array_filter()`, lets you execute a callback function on every array element. If the callback returns `true`, the elements gets pushed to a new array, which is returned at the end:

```
function testVowels(char) {
  return (/[aeiou]/i).test(char);
}

var input = ["a", "b", "c", "d", "e"];
var output = input.filter(testVowels);

output.join(', '); // "a, e"
```

Testing the Array Content

Two new methods, `every()` and `some()`, let you iterate over all array elements and return a boolean, whether or not the array elements satisfy a check you provide in a callback.

Say you want to check if an array contains even numbers. The check will be:

```
function isEven(num) {
  return num % 2 === 0;
}
```

And the tests:

```
// Are *all* of the numbers even?
[1, 2, 4].every(isEven); // false

// Are at least some (or even one) of the numbers even?
[1, 2, 4].some(isEven); // true
```

Map/Reduce

Similar to PHP's `array_map()` and `array_reduce()`, in ES5 you have `Array.proto type.map()` and `Array.prototype.reduce()`, plus one more `Array.prototype.re duceRight()`.

`map()` returns a new array where each element has been changed by your custom call-back function.

Here's a function that turns a character into its HTML entity form:

```
function entity(char) {
  return "&#" + char.charCodeAt(0) + ";";
}
```

Now let's apply it to all elements of an array:

```
var input = ['a', 'b', 'c'];
var out = input.map(entity);
out; // ["&#97;", "&#98;", "&#99;"]
```

`Array.prototype.reduce()` takes an array and reduces it to a single value, using a callback function.

Say you want to sum all numbers in an array and add 100 to the result. So you start with 100 and iteratively add the next value to the running sum:

```
function sum(running_sum, value, index, array) {
  console.log(arguments);
  return running_sum + value;
}

[1, 2, 3].reduce(sum, 100); // 106
```

During the iteration, you'll see in the console:

```
[100, 1, 0, Array[3]]
[101, 2, 1, Array[3]]
[103, 3, 2, Array[3]]
```

`Array.prototype.reduceRight()` is the same, only it loops the array elements from right to left, meaning it starts with the last elements and moves down.

In this example, the result is the same, but you see different output in the console:

```
[1, 2, 3].reduceRight(sum, 100); // 106
```

And the output is:

```
[100, 3, 2, Array[3]]
[103, 2, 1, Array[3]]
[105, 1, 0, Array[3]]
```

String Trimming

Similar to PHP's `trim()` function, ES5 introduces `String.prototype.trim()`:

```
" hello ".trim(); // "hello"
```

And this is the only addition in ES5 related to strings.

 Some environments also offer `trimLeft()` and `trimRight()`, but these are not part of the standard.

New in Date

Three new methods are added to working with dates.

`Date.now()` is a shorter way to do `(new Date()).getTime()` or `+new Date()`. It returns the current timestamp:

```
Date.now(); // 1327943271496

Date.now() === +new Date(); // true
```

`Date.prototype.toISOString()` is another string formatting function:

```
var date = new Date(2012, 11, 31);
date.toDateString(); // "Mon Dec 31 2012"
date.toISOString();  // "2012-12-31T08:00:00.000Z"
```

`toISOString()` is handy for representing dates in JSON format and is used by `JSON.stringify()`, which you'll see later. In fact, there is `Date.prototype.toJSON()`, which returns the same as `toISOString()`:

```
var today = new Date();
today.toJSON() === today.toISOString(); // true
```

Function.prototype.bind()

Since functions are objects that can be passed around, and `this` inside a function depends on how the function is called, it makes it somewhat risky to use `this` with a certainty that it is what you expect it to be. Consider this example:

```
var breakfast = {
  drink: "coffee",
  eat: "bacon",
  my: function () {
    return this.drink + " & " + this.eat;
  }
};

breakfast.my(); // "coffee & bacon"
```

No surprises here. However, you may want a new reference, say:

```
var morning = breakfast.my;
morning(); // "undefined & undefined"
```

In this case, `this` is the global object and there are no `drink` or `eat` properties. But you can bind `my()` method to the `breakfast` object and have it work as expected:

```
var morning = breakfast.my.bind(breakfast);
morning(); // "coffee & bacon"
```

JSON

To wrap up the discussion of ECMAScript 5, let's take a look at the JSON object. It's an addition to ES5 that standardizes what's already implemented in all browsers, including IE8+. JSON stands for "JavaScript Object Notation" and is a data exchange format that uses JavaScript object and array literals to encode arbitrary data.

JSON has two (unfortunately named) methods—`stringify()` and `parse()`—which correspond to PHP's `json_encode()` and `json_decode()`:

```
JSON.stringify({hello: "world"});        // '{"hello":"world"}'
JSON.parse('{"hello":"world"}').hello; // "world"
```

In environments that don't support JSON natively, you can use the shim available here (*http://json.org*).

Shims

"Shims," or "polyfills," are a way to support new APIs in older environments. Since in JavaScript you can change built-in objects and prototypes, you can emulate the new APIs. Here's an example of a shim:

```
if (!Date.now) {
  Date.now = function () {
    return new Date().getTime();
  };
}
```

or:

```
// source:
// https://developer.mozilla.org/en-US/docs/JavaScript/Reference/
//                          Global_Objects/String/Trim
if (!String.prototype.trim) {
  String.prototype.trim = function () {
    return this.replace(/^\s+|\s+$/g, '');
  };
}
```

As you can see, the shims are often small, and you can have them load before your first line of code, thus enabling legacy browsers to handle the new and shiny features.

Be aware that there are some features you can't shim (e.g., strict mode and all methods that deal with property descriptors).

To check which features are supported among browsers, consult this site (*http://kangax.github.com/es5-compat-table/*).

CHAPTER 7

JavaScript Patterns

Now that you know about JavaScript's syntax and built-in APIs, as well as the special treatment of functions and the existence of prototypes, let's take a look at some common JavaScript patterns. These are not necessarily the design patterns from the Gang of Four's book (although there are a few at the end, for good measure), but mostly patterns specific to organizing your code when creating a larger application.

For example, JavaScript doesn't have namespaces, modules, or private properties, but these are all features that are easy to replicate.

You'll notice that most of the time, the solutions to a lot of problems boil down to interesting uses of functions, which is why understanding functions, closures, and scope is critical to mastering JavaScript.

Private Properties

In ES5, you can use property descriptors to limit access to certain properties, but you can't do anything like this in ES3. So how do you create private properties that no one is allowed to touch?

The solution is to use a closure and not expose the variables you want to keep private. These will not be exactly private *properties* of an object, but they will be private nevertheless.

An example of using a closure for privacy was discussed in "Immediate Functions" on page 47. But the topic is worth reviewing and expanding. A common pattern of using a closure to define an object is like this:

```
var my = (function () {
  return {
    hi: 1,
    bye: 2
  };
```

```
}());

my.hi; // 1
```

At first sight, the end result is not different than doing the following:

```
var my = {
  hi: 1,
  bye: 2
};

my.hi; // 1
```

For simple objects, the two examples are the same. But with the first one, you can hide important data inside the closure:

```
var my = (function () {
  var hidden_private = 42;
  return {
    hi: 1 + hidden_private,
    bye: 2 + hidden_private
  };
}());

my.bye; // 44
```

Here the `hidden_private` variable is tucked inside the closure (the immediate function) and there's no access to it from the outside. For all intents and purposes, it can be considered a private property of the object `my`.

Private Methods

Just like with regular variables, you can also put functions inside the closure. They have access to everything inside it, so they can access the publicly returned properties as well as the local (private) variables. You can consider using such functions as you would use PHP's *private methods*.

Here's an example where you have a `special()` function, which can access both the value of `hidden_private` as well as the `public_api` object, which is returned and accessible outside the closure:

```
var my = (function () {
  var hidden_private = 42;

  function special() {
    return Number(public_api.hi) + hidden_private;
  }

  var public_api = {
    hi: 1,
    get: function () {
      return special();
```

```
      }
    };

    return public_api;
  }());

  my.hi;        // 1
  my.get();     // 43
  my.hi = 100;  // 100
  my.get();     // 142
```

As you can see, the property `hi` can be modified outside the closure, and the method `get()`, which internally calls `special()`, will still work with the updated value.

Exposing Private Objects

In the example in the previous section, the private function `special()` was given public access:

```
var public_api = {
  hi: 1,
  get: function () {
    return special();
  }
};
```

Another way to do so is as follows:

```
var public_api = {
  hi: 1,
  get: special
};
```

The second example is simpler and works fine for most use cases, but it does come with a certain risk. Since `special()` is a function, it's also an object, and because objects are passed by reference, this means that code outside the closure can modify the properties of that object.

Let's consider a simpler example:

```
var my = (function () {
  function special() {
    return "ohai";
  }

  var public_api = {
    get: special
  };

  return public_api;
}());
```

You can call the get() method directly or by using its call method:

```
my.get();      // "ohai"
my.get.call(); // "ohai"
```

However, it's completely legal to overwrite the call method with something else, which is not even a method:

```
my.get.call = "not so special";
```

The next time you try call(), you'll get an error because it's no longer callable:

```
my.get.call(); // TypeError: call is not a function
```

So you have to be careful when you expose private objects publicly.

Returning Private Arrays

The previous example showed how to expose a function, but you can expose arrays (also objects) or other objects.

Say you have a private array and you want to give read (but not write) access to it. Doing the following looks like it should be a good enough protection:

```
var my = (function () {

  var days = ["Mo", "Tu", "We", "Th", "Fr", "Sa", "Su"];

  return {
    getDays: function () {
      return days;
    }
  };
}());
```

Outside the closure, you get the days just fine, and you don't have a direct way to access the private days variable:

```
my.getDays(); // ["Mo", "Tu", "We", "Th", "Fr", "Sa", "Su"]
```

However, you get *indirect* access because the array is an object and it's passed by reference, which you can use to add another element to the array:

```
my.getDays().push('Js'); // We need one JavaScript day each week!
```

And it works!

```
my.getDays(); // ["Mo", "Tu", "We", "Th", "Fr", "Sa", "Su", "Js"]
```

A way to protect the array is not to return it directly, but to return a copy of it. Using the fact that slice() will return a new array, you can use it as a general copy-making tool:

```
var my = (function () {

  var days = ["Mo", "Tu", "We", "Th", "Fr", "Sa", "Su"];

  return {
    getDays: function () {
      return days.slice();
    }
  };
}());
```

An attempt to sneak in an extra day in the weekend will now be unsuccessful:

```
my.getDays().push('Js');
my.getDays(); // ["Mo", "Tu", "We", "Th", "Fr", "Sa", "Su"]
```

If days were not an array but an object with some unknown properties (some properties may be other objects, some may be arrays), you would need to create a deep copy of it and return it.

Deep Copy via JSON

The simplest way to create a deep copy is to JSON-encode then decode the object. This may not be the most efficient way, especially in browsers that don't support JSON natively, but it's certainly short:

```
var my = (function () {

  var stuff = {
    a: {
      b: [1, 2]
    }
  };

  return {
    getStuff: function () {
      return JSON.parse(JSON.stringify(stuff));
    }
  };
}());
```

Accessing stuff for reading, but not writing:

```
my.getStuff().a.b.toString(); // "1,2"

// change
my.getStuff().a.b.push(3);
my.getStuff().a.c = "Ch-ch-changin";

// test changes?
my.getStuff().a.b.toString(); // "1,2"
typeof my.getStuff().a.c;      // "undefined"
```

To make getStuff() more efficient, you can use an immediate function that precomputes the JSON encode/decode and returns a snapshot of stuff at the time of definition:

```javascript
var my = (function () {

  var stuff = {
    a: {
      b: [1, 2]
    }
  };

  return {
    getStuff: function () {
      var snap = JSON.parse(JSON.stringify(stuff));
      return function () {
        return snap;
      };
    }(),

    getRealStuff: function () {
      return JSON.parse(JSON.stringify(stuff));
    }
  };
}());
```

Here you have an immediate anonymous function (notice the () at the end of get Stuff()) that clones stuff into snap. Then this function returns a new function that simply returns the existing snap. Later, when you do my.getStuff(), it's the inner function that is executed, and it has access to snap because both snap and the inner function were created inside the closure created by the immediate (wrapper) function.

Now calls to getStuff() return snap, which is not protected via a clone. Therefore, snap can be tampered with, but the important stuff stays safe:

```javascript
my.getStuff().a.b.push(3);
my.getStuff().a.b.toString();       // "1,2,3"
my.getRealStuff().a.b.toString(); // "1,2"
```

Of course, since in ES3 everything is mutable, nothing really prevents you from overwriting or even wiping out completely the public API getStuff() and getReal Stuff() and destroying all your hard work of carefully protecting private properties and methods. In other words, if you want to shoot yourself in the foot, there are certainly easy ways to do so:

```javascript
my.getRealStuff = function () {
  return "or don't!";
};
delete my.getStuff; // true

my.getRealStuff(); // "or don't!"
my.getStuff();     // Error: no such method
```

Revealing Pattern

Related to the question of privacy is the so-called *revealing* pattern. The idea is that when you provide an object, you make everything private by default and at the end you decide which parts to *reveal* by making them public.

If you were to rewrite the previous example using the revealing pattern, you would end up with something similar to the following snippet:

```
var my = (function () {

  var stuff = {
    a: {
      b: [1, 2]
    }
  };

  function encodeStuff() {
    return JSON.parse(JSON.stringify(stuff));
  }

  var getStuff = function () {
    var snap = encodeStuff();
    return function () {
      return snap;
    };
  }();

  // Revelation happens here
  return {
    getStuff: getStuff,
    getRealStuff: encodeStuff
  };
}());
```

Some things to note here:

- Everything is private until the very last `return` statement, where you decide how much you want to reveal in the form of a public API.
- You don't need to use the same function names for public/private—the public `getRealStuff` is actually the private `encodeStuff`.
- One private function can use another private function internally.
- It's up to you to decide how to treat the `name` property of the functions you reveal.

Testing:

```
// getStuff was defined with anonymous function expression
my.getStuff.name; // ""
```

```
// encodeStuff was defined with a function declaration, so it bleeds
// into the public API, which may or may not be a concern
my.getRealStuff.name; // "encodeStuff"
```

A drawback of that pattern is that it is difficult to discern the private from the public methods while reading the code. You have to scroll down to see which methods are exposed. Possible solutions include exposing right after creating the function or using comments to signal your intention to make the function a public one.

Constants

Some JavaScript environments provide the special const statement, which can be used instead of var:

```
const PI = 3.14;
```

But even in ES5 there is no such thing as a constant. You can work around this limitation by either using a convention or introducing a utility. However, both of these options have drawbacks (a convention is not enforceable, and a utility is overkill for most tasks). If you're considering a convention, be aware that the common convention is to use ALLCAPS for constant names. If you go with a constant utility, you can use a closure where you define your own private repository for all your constants.

Let's create an object constant that implements the following methods (mimicking the PHP's functions that deal with constants):

- define()
- defined()
- constant()

```
var constant = (function () {
  var constants = {}, // All constants go here
      ownProp = Object.prototype.hasOwnProperty, // Shorthand
      allowed = {     // Only primitive types accepted
        string: 1,
        number: 1,
        boolean: 1
      };

  return {

    define: function (name, value) {
      if (this.defined(name)) {
        return false;
      }
      if (!ownProp.call(allowed, typeof value)) {
        return false;
      }
```

```
          constants[name] = value;
          return true;
        },

        defined: function (name) {
          return ownProp.call(constants, name);
        },

        constant: function (name) {
          if (this.defined(name)) {
            return constants[name];
          }
          return null;
        }

      };
    }());
```

Using the `constants` object:

```
constant.constant('hi');     // null, it doesn't exist
constant.defined('hi');      // false
constant.define('hi', 'ho'); // true

// Attempt to redefine a constant should fail
constant.define('hi', 'hoho'); // false
constant.constant('hi');       // "ho"
```

`define()` checks the type of value to be stored as a constant and only allows primitive types. That makes it easier not to deal with the cloning and matches PHP where you cannot have an object or an array stored as a constant.

Namespaces

There are no namespaces in JavaScript, but you can simply use properties of an object for this purpose.

A common approach is to define a single global variable in your application or library. Then everything else you do becomes a property of that global object.

Let's call the global `APP`.

 Using uppercase is a convention you can adopt for global variables to make them stand out. That conflicts with PHP's convention to use uppercase for constants.

If you want to define `constants` and `my`, make them properties of `APP`:

```
var APP = {};

// Define my
APP.my = {
  // ...
};

// Constants
APP.constant = {
  define: function () {
    // ...
  }
  // ...
};

// Something else
APP.my.more = {
  // ...
};
```

Since APP.my and APP.constant are distinct, potentially big chunks of functionality, it would be wise to implement them in different files for simplicity. (Your build process will then merge the files and minify them for performance purposes in production.) These chunks of code may be included dynamically under different circumstances, and you may not know if constant, for example, wasn't already defined. If you blindly do APP.constant = {}, then you wipe out any other previously created property with the same name (and in this case, you lose all your constants). That why it's important to check before you add a big new property:

```
if (!APP.constant) {
  APP.constant = {
    // ..
  };
}
```

But since this can quickly become tedious, especially for deeply nested properties, it would be nice to have a general-purpose namespace() function:

```
// Argh!
if (APP && APP.my && !APP.my.more) {
  APP.my.more = {};
}

// Better
APP.namespace('APP.my.more');
```

Here's an example implementation of a generic namespace() function:

```
var APP = {
  namespace: function (ns) {
    var parts = ns.split('.'),
        parent = APP,
```

```
      i;

    // Strip redundant global
    if (parts[0] === "APP") {
      parts = parts.slice(1);
    }

    for (i = 0; i < parts.length; i++) {
      // Create a property if it doesn't exist
      if (typeof parent[parts[i]] === "undefined") {
        parent[parts[i]] = {};
      }
      parent = parent[parts[i]];
    }
    return parent;
  }
};
```

Now you can do:

```
var my = APP.namespace('APP.my');
my === APP.my; // true

APP.namespace('my.more');
typeof APP.my.more; // "object"
```

Modules

There is no concept of modules in JavaScript, but the name *module pattern* is often used to refer to a combination of several things already discussed in the chapter, namely:

- Namespaces to define each module as a property of a single global object.
- An immediate function that wraps the whole module definition and provides privacy, if required, as well as a place for any temporary variables used to define and initialize the module.
- The immediate function returns an object (or a constructor function if you're so inclined), which reveals a public API.

The overall skeleton of a new module would look like this:

```
APP.namespace('my.shiny').module = (function () {

  // Short names for dependencies
  var shiny = APP.my.shiny;

  // Local/private variables
  var i, j;

  // Private functions
  function hidden() {}
```

```
    // Public API
    return {
      willYouUseMe: function () {
        return "Yups";
      }
    };

  }());
```

Using the new module:

```
APP.my.shiny.module.willYouUseMe(); // "Yups"
```

CommonJS Modules

Another approach to organizing your code into modules is provided by the CommonJS specification. CommonJS is not a standard established by a standards body such as Ecma International or W3C, but is a community-driven project aiming to have developers agree on common practices for writing cross-environment JavaScript. The modules specification is just one (albeit the most popular) of the subprojects within CommonJS.

There are currently no browsers that implement CommonJS modules natively, but there are environments and frameworks that provide module support. One of the most prominent environments with CommonJS support is NodeJS.

Defining a CommonJS Module

The following snippet is a definition of a bare-bones CommonJS module:

```
// Private variables
var i, j;

// Private functions
function hidden() {}

// Public API
exports.sayHi = function () {
  return "hi!";
};
```

What do you have here?

- There's no need for an immediate function wrapper.

- Private variables and functions are simply defined as you would define a global. However, the CommonJS implementation takes care of making these variables local, so everything you do is local by default.

- You add properties to a special `exports` object. Anything you add to `exports` becomes your module's publicly accessible API.

Using a CommonJS Module

How do you use this module from your program or from another module? In NodeJS, the filename of the module serves as a module identifier. So if you save the definition from the previous snippet in a file called *hi.js*, you can then use it like so:

```
var hi = require("./hi.js");
hi.sayHi(); // "hi!"
```

As you can see, the other CommonJS magic (in addition to `exports`) is the function called `require()`. It takes a module identifier, finds and evaluates the required module, and returns the `exports` object from that module (Figure 7-1).

```
@ O O                tests — node — 80×24
stoyanstefanov:tests stoyanstefanov$ cat hi.js
// private variables
var i, j;

// private functions
function hidden() {}

// public API
exports.sayHi = function() {
    return "hi!";
};
stoyanstefanov:tests stoyanstefanov$ node
> var hi = require('./hi');
> hi.sayHi();
'hi!'
> ▌
```

Figure 7-1. Defining and using a CommonJS module in NodeJS console

 Depending on the environment, you may be able to specify the module identifier in a different manner (e.g., in NodeJS, the `.js` is optional). In others, the module identifier may just be a string, not a file path. When you define your module with `exports`, you have the object `module` as well, and you can specify a `module.id` to identify the module.

Using `require()`, you get the module's `exports` object and assign it to a local variable, which doesn't need to have the same name. This is also fine:

```
var bye = require("./hi");
```

You can export several properties and get a handle to a specific property when you use `require()`. For example, you can assign the `sayHi()` directly to a variable:

```
var hey = require("./hi").sayHi;
hey(); // "hi!"
```

As you can see, using CommonJS is much simpler and friendlier than the module pattern's namespaces and closures. All the hassle is taken care of for you, and you have at your disposal the `require()` function and the `exports` object.

Using an Agnostic Module

If you want to create a portable piece of JavaScript (say, an open source library) and you don't know whether it will be used in a CommonJS environment or not, you can still support both by:

- Defining a simple namespace/object
- Adding all your stuff there
- Checking for `exports` and making your public API a property of `exports`

For example, here is how you would do it:

```
// Single global/namespace
var JS4PHP = JS4PHP || {};

// Define the functionality of your `utils` module
JS4PHP.utils = {
  isOdd: function (num) {
    return num % 2 !== 0;
  }
};

// CommonJS?
if (typeof exports === "object") {
  exports.utils = JS4PHP.utils;
}
```

This way, non-CommonJS environments can simply load your code and use the longer namespaced method call:

```
JS4PHP.utils.isOdd(10); // false
```

This sort of namespacing is longer than just `utils.isOdd()`, but it provides some degree of certainty that the user of your `JS4PHP` utility doesn't already have a variable with the same name in their code.

In CommonJS environments, your module can be used without worrying about globals and namespaces. For example:

```
require('./utils').utils.isOdd(11); // true
```

AMD

Another idea of implementing modules in JavaScript is called AMD, or Asynchronous Module Definition. It's similar to CommonJS in the way it uses a `require()` function to include a module inside another module or program.

But while CommonJS doesn't bother with the details of how a module is defined (it's the environment's task), the AMD pattern describes a function called `define()`.

So defining a module looks like:

```
define('hi', ['hello'], function () {
  // Private variables
  var i, j;

  // Private functions
  function hidden() {}

  // Public API
  return {
    sayHi: function () {
      return "hi!";
    }
  };
});
```

The function that defines the module is the same as with CommonJS, only you simply `return` the public API instead of assigning it to an `exports` object.

The first argument to `define()` is the new module name and the second is an array of dependencies (other modules the new module needs).

Using the `hi` module in your program looks like:

```
require(['hi'], function (hi) {
  hi.sayHi(); // "hi!"
});
```

The first argument to `require()` is a list of modules you need; the second is a callback function that is called when this module is available.

"When available" because AMD worries about loading modules asynchronously (the A in the name). Imagine you load a page that only needs three modules. Then the user interacts with the page, and your program requires another module that is not currently loaded. Your AMD helper library takes care of fetching your additional module and invoking your callback when the module is available.

The most popular open source AMD utility at the time of writing is RequireJS (*http://requirejs.org*).

Design Patterns

For dessert, let's consider a few design patterns from the Gang of Four's book. Bear in mind that patterns designed for static, strongly typed, class-based languages could be trivial to implement or unnecessary in a language such as JavaScript.

Singleton

The singleton pattern ensures that there's only one object of a certain class and provides a single global access to it. JavaScript doesn't have classes, so a single instance of a class doesn't make sense. Additionally, all objects are unique, so the term *singleton* in JavaScript can be just another name for *an object*:

```
var singleton = {a: 1};
var another = {a: 1};
singleton === another; // false
```

As you can see, `singleton` is already a unique object.

 Sometimes when people say "singleton" in JavaScript they mean an object created using the module pattern.

Singletons with constructors

But what if your team is so attached to the concept of classes that they want to create all the objects with constructor functions? In other words, you're looking for something that behaves like this:

```
function Single() {
  // magic!
}

var a = new Single();
var b = new Single();
a === b; // true
```

Since the goal is to have a single hidden *instance* (object), you can get a little help from an old friend—the closure created by an immediate function:

```
var Single = (function () {
  var instance;

  function Single() {
    // Own properties
```

```
    this.say_what = "Hi";
  }

  // Prototype properties
  Single.prototype.say = function () {
    return this.say_what;
  };

  return function () {
    if (!instance) {
      instance = new Single();
    }
    return instance;
  };

}());
```

Here the `instance` is protected inside a closure. The same closure contains the local `Single` constructor function, which works like a regular constructor where you can add properties either to `this` or to `Single.prototype`. It doesn't really matter which way you choose: the benefit of the prototype is a single definition for all instances, but in this case you only have a single instance anyway.

The immediate function returns a function that is assigned to the global `Single` variable. Then you can call this this global with `new`:

```
// Get an instance
var a = new Single();
a.say(); // "Hi"
```

Only the first call to `new Single` creates a new object. From then on, the private in stance is returned:

```
// Get another instance, which should be the same
var b = new Single();
b.say(); // "Hi"
```

```
// Check if the singleton worked
a === b;          // true
a.say === b.say; // true
```

For simplicity, there was a global `Single`, but it doesn't need to be global; you can always create the constructor in a namespace like `APP.Single`:

```
APP.Single = (function () {
  // ....
}());

var mysingle = new APP.Single();
mysingle.say(); // "Hi"
```

Factory

The factory method pattern allows you to defer the object creation to more specific subclasses/constructors. This allows you to decide at runtime which class/constructor you'll use to create an object. You usually pass a string to a static factory() or build() method, and this method takes care of finding the right class to instantiate.

In PHP, you commonly use a prefix to namespace your classes, or, in newer versions, use a real namespace. For example:

```php
// PHP

// Specific implementations
class Polygon_Triangle {}
class Polygon_Square {}
class Polygon_Circle {}

// Where the factory lives
class Polygon {
  static function factory($name) {
    $class = "Polygon_" . ucfirst(strtolower($name));
    if (class_exists($class)) {
      return new $class;
    }
    throw new Exception($class . " doesn't exist");
  }
}

// Usage
$tri = Polygon::factory('triangle');
echo get_class($tri); // "Polygon_Triangle"

// Throws an Exception, there's no Polygon_Rectangle
$rect = Polygon::factory('rectangle');
```

The most important part here is return new $class;. PHP allows you to create instances of classes that are not known in advance. In other languages, you might need to have a long switch statement listing all known classes.

In JavaScript, you can make Polygon an object and use it as a namespace as well as a place to keep your static factory() method:

```javascript
// JavaScript
var Polygon = {
  factory: function (name) {
    var constr = name.charAt(0).toUpperCase() + name.slice(1).toLowerCase();
    if (Polygon[constr]) {
      return new Polygon[constr]();
    }
    throw new Error("Polygon." + name + " doesn't exist");
  }
```

```
};

// Specific implementations
Polygon.Triangle = function () {};
Polygon.Square   = function () {};
Polygon.Circle   = function () {};

// Usage
var tri = Polygon.factory('triangle');
tri instanceof Polygon.Triangle;  // true

new Polygon.factory('Rectangle'); // Error: Polygon.Rectangle doesn't exist
```

There's no special trick or syntax here; it's about simply accessing a property using the square bracket notation. And since you know this property is a constructor function, you can return a new object with new Polygon[constr].

Decorator

The decorator pattern lets you augment an object's functionality at runtime while preserving the interface. It's yet another alternative to inheritance.

Imagine you need some text-handling objects created by a Text() constructor that deals with user input:

```
function Text(txt) {
  this.input = txt;
}

Text.prototype.get = function () {
  return this.input;
};
```

Using this constructor is simple:

```
var my = new Text('hello,_world_!wassup?');
my.get(); // "hello,_world_!wassup?"
```

The returned text doesn't look too pretty though. It could use some decoration.

Decoration API

The decoration API looks like this:

```
my.decorate('punctuation'); // Fix spaces after punctuation
my.decorate('italics');     // Turn _ into <i>

my.get(); // "hello, <i>world</i>! wassup? "
```

Using the decorators, your program can decide at any time which decoration is appropriate for the given task and enhance the object my with extra functionality. Also, the order of the decoration may be important (e.g., a decorator that escapes HTML should run before the one that adds HTML tags such as <i>).

In effect, your program chains decorators one after the other. Each decorator should therefore work with the result of the previous decorator in the chain.

Adding decorators

Let's use `Text()` as a namespace and add all the decorators there:

```
Text.decorators = {};
```

The first decorator adds missing spaces after punctuation:

```
Text.decorators.punctuation = {
  get: function (text) {
    return text.replace(/([;,!\?])\s*/g, '$1 ');
  }
};
```

Here you have a `punctuation` object with a single method. This method receives the output of the decorator that comes before it in the call chain and further modifies the text.

Same for the `italics` object:

```
Text.decorators.italics = {
  get: function (text) {
    return text.replace(/(_)(.*?)(_)/g, '<i>$2</i>');
  }
};
```

And finally, an `escape` object:

```
Text.decorators.escape = {
  get: function (text) {
    return text.replace(/&/g, '&amp;').
                replace(/</g, '&lt;').
                replace(/>/g, '&gt;');
  }
};
```

decorate() and get()

Now that the API is clear and the decorators exist, it's time for the `decorate()` method.

First, you need to slightly modify the `Text()` constructor so it maintains a list of decorators currently requested:

```
function Text(txt) {
  this.input = txt;
  this.decorators_list = [];
}
```

The decorate() method is actually simply appending to the list of required decorators:

```
Text.prototype.decorate = function (decorator) {
  this.decorators_list.push(decorator);
};
```

The most intelligence will be hidden in the core get() method, which you rewrite to look like so:

```
Text.prototype.get = function () {
    var txt = this.input,
      max = this.decorators_list.length,
      name;
    for (var i = 0; i < max; i++) {
      name = this.decorators_list[i];
      txt = Text.decorators[name].get(txt);
    }
    return txt;
};
```

As you can see, this method loops over all requested decorators and calls each one's get(), passing the result of the previous.

More testing:

```
my.input = "_hi_,ho,_ho_";
my.get(); // "<i>hi</i>, ho, <i>ho</i>"
```

You can always add more decorators:

```
my.decorate('escape');
my.get(); // "&lt;i&gt;hi&lt;/i&gt;, ho, &lt;i&gt;ho&lt;/i&gt;"
```

This was just one example implementation of the decorator pattern. It didn't use any inheritance, but you can have another implementation that sets up an inheritance chain, as opposed to a call chain.

Documentation and Testing

Let's wrap up this chapter and the book with a few words about documentation and testing in JavaScript.

Manual

One of the really strong points of PHP is its great manual (*http://php.net*), especially with all the user-contributed comments. No exact equivalent exists for JavaScript. Still, the Mozilla Developer Network (MDN) has an excellent online resource (*https://devel oper.mozilla.org/en/JavaScript/Reference/*) you can consult. Even though it's about Mozilla and Firefox, there are often notes about IE and other browsers where necessary.

For IE-specific flavors, your best resource is the MSDN site (*http://msdn.micro soft.com/*).

And, of course, you can always consult the ECMA-262 specs (*http://www.ecma-international.org/publications/standards/Ecma-262.htm*).

Documenting Your Code

If you're familiar with PHPDoc or JavaDoc, you'll be happy to learn that you can use the same idea for inline commenting in JavaScript:

```
/**
 * Sums two numbers
 *
 * @param {Number} a First number
 * @param {Number} b Second number
 * @return {Number} The sum
 */
function sum(a, b) {
  return a + b;
}
```

There are several tools you can use to generate documentation from comments, including JSDoc Toolkit (*http://code.google.com/p/jsdoc-toolkit/*) and YUIDoc (*http://yuilibrary.com/projects/yuidoc/*).

In JavaScript, where you have more than one choice to do certain tasks (e.g., inheritance), the documentation system may not be able to deduce the purpose of a piece of code, so it usually provides you with special new tags such as @inherits, @class, or @constructor that you can use to declare your intentions.

Unit Testing

There are several projects that help you unit test your JavaScript code. One example is Jasmine (*http://pivotal.github.com/jasmine/*), which has a plain-English type of API.

Let's say you want to unit test the following constructor function:

```
function Text(txt) {
  this.input = txt;
}

Text.prototype.get = function () {
  return this.input;
};
```

Your unit test file would look like this:

```
describe("Text", function () {

  // first test
```

```
  it("creates objects", function () {
    expect(new Text("wee").input).toBe("wee");
  });

  // second test
  it("can get back the input", function () {
    // setup
    var t = new Text("hello");

    // multiple assertions
    expect(t.get).toBeDefined();
    expect(t.put).toBeUndefined();
    expect(t.get()).toBe('hello');
  });

});
```

Besides Jasmine, you have more options to pick from when it comes to unit testing.

For testing user interactions in a browser, you can use Selenium (*http://seleniumhq.org/*).

There's also a tool called JSCoverage (*http://siliconforks.com/jscoverage/*), which you can run to instrument your code before running the unit tests and then get an idea of the code coverage of your tests.

JSLint

JSLint (*http://jslint.com*) is tool that inspects your code statically to look for potentially dangerous patterns as well as simple things like indentation and missing semicolons. Since JavaScript is not compiled, some errors are easily masked, and JSLint helps you uncover some of these before the code goes to production.

JSLint has been ported to many environments, and is available as a plug-in to many IDEs and text editors. You can easily integrate it with your text editor and run it on every file save, which will give you a greater confidence in the quality of your code.

Some developers consider JSLint too restrictive and opinionated, but it has quite a few options, so you can tweak and turn off specific checks you disagree with. A similar tool called JSHint (*http://jshint.com*) allows finer-grained control over which checks you want to turn on. Another linter is JavaScript Lint (*http://www.javascriptlint.com/*), based on Mozilla's SpiderMonkey JavaScript engine.

Linting This Book

All of the examples in this book were continuously run through JSHint to assure high quality of the code samples and prevent regressions in late-stage tweaks. However, since there are some intentional errors and bad practices for educational purposes, there are some JSHint checks that were turned off. Now that you know so much about JavaScript, you'll find these behind-the-scenes glimpses interesting. Here is the full list of JSHint options used for checking the book samples:

```
var lintopts = {
  indent: 2,        // Two spaces for indentation
  plusplus: false,  // Allows ++ and --
  browser: true,    // Assumes some common browser globals exist,
                    // such as `document`
  node: true,       // Assumes the code can run in node.js
                    // and globals such as `global` are defined
  expr: true,       // OK to have expressions that seemingly do nothing,
                    // such as `a; // true`, which the samples use to show
                    // result values
  loopfunc: true,   // Allows definition of a function in a loop
                    // for educational purposes (in the part about closures)
  newcap: false,    // Allows calling constructors (capitalized functions)
                    // without `new`—again, just for educational purposes
  proto: true       // Allows using `__proto__`, which is great for understanding
                    // prototypes, although it's not supported in all browsers
};
```

 For more details on how the code snippets in the book were unit tested and lint checked, see this blog post (*http://www.jspatterns.com/unit-testing-in-asciidoc/*).

Index

Symbols

!! operator, 23
" (double quote), 11
$$() function, 11
$() function, 10
$GLOBALS (PHP), equivalent of, 73
&& operator, 24
' (single quote), 11
() operator, 47–50
+ operator
    string concatenation and, 23
    type casting with, 23
. (dot) notation, 15
    object properties and, 62
; (semicolon) operator, 31
== operator, 16
=== operator, 16–17
__proto__ property, 65
|| operator, 24

A

AMD, 127–128
anonymous function, 32
apply() method, 30
    inheritance and, 71
arguments
    functions as, 50–53
    optional, 29

    unknown number of, 28–29
arguments array-like object
    func_get_args() method (PHP) vs., 28
Array prototype, 81–87
    every() method, 109
    filter() method, 108
    forEach() method, 108
    indexOf() method, 108
    length property, 82
    map() method, 109
    reduce() method, 109
    reduceRight() method, 109
    some() method, 109
Array.prototype
    isArray() method, 107
    lastIndexOf() method, 108
arrays, 13–15
    . (dot) notation and, 15
    adding elements to, 14
    associative, 15
    declaring, 13
    delete operator, 15
    properties of objects in, 15
    returning private, 116–117
    testing elements of, 109
    transversing with for-in loops, 20
    walking elements of, 108
array_filter() function (PHP), 109
array_map() function (PHP), 109

We'd like to hear your suggestions for improving our indexes. Send email to index@oreilly.com.

N

named function expression, 31
namespaces
  agnostic modules and, 126
  classes, in PHP, 130
  implementing, 121–123
NaN property (global object), 74
new operator, 55
NFE, 31
Node, 6–7
NodeJS environment, 124
null value type, 13
number values
  declaring, 11
  hexadecimal, 12
  octal, 12
  scientific notation, 12
  typeof operator and, 12
Number() constructor, 95–96

O

Object API (ES5), 103–107
  create() method, 103
  defineProperties() method, 104
  defineProperty() method, 104
  getOwnPropertyDescriptor() method, 104
  getPrototypeOf() method, 107
  looping, 106
  mutations, restricting, 105
object literals, 60–63
  accessing properties of, 61
  as associative arrays, 64
  methods in, 62
object oriented programming, 55–72
  constructors/classes, 55–59
  fancy arrays, 63–64
  inheritance, 66–72
  object literals, 60–63
  own properties, 64–66
  prototypes, 59–60
Object prototype, 77–81
  constructor property of, 81
  hasOwnProperty() method, 80
  isPrototypeOf() method, 81
  propertyIsEnumerable() method, 80
  toLocaleString() method, 79
  toString() method and, 78
  valueOf() method, 80

objects
  begetting, 69
  private, exposing, 115–116
  __proto__ property, 65
octal number values, 12
operators, 21–25

P

parameters, default, 27–28
() operator, 47–50
parseFloat() global function, 75
parseInt() global function, 75
pattern design, 128–133
  decorator, 131–133
  factory, 130–131
  singleton, 128–129
patterns, 113–136
  AMD modules, 127–128
  CommonJS module, 124–127
  constants, 120–121
  designing, 128–133
  documentation, 133–134
  module, 123–124
  namespaces, implementing as, 121–123
  revealing, 119–120
  testing, 134–136
performance, 19
php -a and node REPL, 7
polyfils, 112
pop() method (Array.prototypes), 83
preg_match() function (PHP), 95
preg_match_all() function (PHP), 95
private properties, 113–118
  deep copying with JSON, 117–118
  exposing objects, 115–116
  methods, 114–115
  returning private arrays, 116–117
properties
  copying for inheritance, 68
  descriptor objects for, 102
  private, 113–118
propertyIsEnumerable() method (Object constructor), 80
__proto__ property, 65
prototypes, 3
  inheritance via, 66–72
  own properties vs. properties from, 64–66
  this operator vs., 66
push() method (Array.prototypes), 14, 83

unshift() method (Array.prototypes), 84
urldecode() function (PHP), 76
urlencode() function (PHP), 76
URLs, encoding, 76
use keyword (PHP), equivilant to, 36
usort() method (PHP), 85

V

V8 JavaScript Engine (Google), 6
V8Js PHP class, 2–4
value types, 11–13
    null, 13
    number values, 11
    type casting, 23
    undefined, 13
valueOf() method, 80
var keyword, 9
    variable scope and, 10
variables, 9
    defining, 9
    functions as, 31–32
    hoisting, 33–34

references vs. values, retaining, 44
retaining scope, 43
scope and the var keyword, 10
scope chain of, 37–47
scope of, 32–33
variables object (functions), 37
void operator, 24

W

WebKit console, 39–42
Windows, built-in JavaScript interpreter for, 5

X

XHTML, 2
XML, 2

Y

YUI (Yahoo User Interface Library), 2
YUIDoc, 134

About the Author

Stoyan Stefanov is a Facebook engineer, ex-Yahoo, architect of the YSlow 2.0 performance tool, and creator of the smush.it image optimization tool.

He's the author of *JavaScript Patterns* (O'Reilly), *Object-Oriented JavaScript* (Packt Publishing), *The Book of Speed* (online), and a contributor to *High Performance JavaScript* (O'Reilly) and *Even Faster Web Sites* (O'Reilly).

Stoyan is a Zend-certified engineer, blogs at phpied.com (*http://www.phpied.com/*) and jspatterns.com (*http://www.jspatterns.com/*), and speaks at conferences and meetups around the world (Velocity, JSConf, Web Directions, and Fronteers, among others).

A Bulgarian-Canadian, Stoyan lives in Los Angeles with his wife and daughters and spends his time biking between home, office, the beach, band practice, flying lessons, and kids' birthday parties.

Colophon

The animal on the cover of *JavaScript for PHP Developers* is an eastern gray squirrel (*Sciurus carolinensis*), which is a tree squirrel native to the eastern and midwestern United States, and to the southern portions of the eastern provinces of Canada. The genus, *Sciurus*, is derived from two Greek words: *skia*, meaning shadow, and *oura*, meaning tail.

As the name suggests, the eastern gray squirrel has predominantly gray fur, but it can also have a brownish color. It has a white underside and a large bushy tail. It is one of very few mammalian species that can descend a tree head-first; it does this by turning its feet so the claws of its hind paws point backward and can grip the tree bark.

Like many members of the *Sciuridae* family, the eastern gray squirrel is a scatter-hoarder: it hoards food in numerous small caches for later recovery. Some caches are quite temporary, especially those made near the site of a sudden abundance of food that can be retrieved within hours or days for reburial in a more secure site. Others are more permanent and are not retrieved until months later. Each squirrel is estimated to make several thousand caches each season. The squirrels have very accurate spatial memory for the locations of these caches, and use distant and nearby landmarks to retrieve them.

As in most other mammals, communication among eastern gray squirrel individuals involves both vocalizations and posturing. The species has a quite varied repertoire of vocalizations, including a squeak similar to that of a mouse, a low-pitched noise, a chatter, and a raspy sound. Other methods of communication include tail flicking. Communications are mainly used in mating season and to ward off predators.

The cover image is from Wood's *Animate Creation*. The cover font is Adobe ITC Garamond. The text font is Adobe Minion Pro; the heading font is Adobe Myriad Condensed; and the code font is Dalton Maag's Ubuntu Mono.

organism, the physiological responses of the animal body according to the form of salt consumed (brine or rock salt), and the uses of rock salt and brine in traditional folk medicine and alimentary practices. He has published on these topics twelve ISI articles and fourteen in other major international journals, and made twelve inventions concerning halochambers and methods for detecting aerosols. Email: ion.sandu@uaic.ro.

Sandra SIVILLI is graduated in Prehistoric and Protohistoric Archaeology at the University of Rome 'La Sapienza' (prof. A. Manfredini), postgraduate in Palethnology. She works from 1998 among Soprintendenza Speciale dei Beni Archeologici of Rome and Soprintendenza per i Beni Archeologici della Puglia; she studies Neolithic settlements in Puglia (South-East Italy), specially the lithic industries and circulation of lithic raw materials (publications 2001 until today), end the environmental and archaeological developments of the lagoon of Maccarese (Roma-Fiumicino) (publications 2004 until today). E-mail: sandra@arkeologia.com.

Ulrich STOCKINGER has been a graduate research assistant at the Archaeological Department of the University of Cologne (Germany) since 2012. He has been working on several projects at the Cologne Digital Archaeology Laboratory such as the iDAI.gazetteer and is currently involved in the research training group 'Archaeology of Pre-Modern Economies'. His Master's thesis enquires the *Produktion, Handel und Konsum von Salz in den Nordwestprovinzen und im angrenzenden Barbaricum* (forthcoming) and has so far been presented at the 6th JIA in Barcelona, the 18th CIAC in Mérida and the 19th EAA Annual Meeting in Pilsen. E-mail: stockinu@uni-koeln.de.

Felix Adrian TENCARIU is researcher at the Interdisciplinary Research Department – Field Science of the "Al. I. Cuza" University (Iaşi, Romania). His main research interests are the Neolithic and Chalcolithic periods in south-eastern Europe, with special emphasis on the different issues and topics of the prehistoric pottery *chaine opératoire*. During his doctoral studies and afterwards, his research was oriented towards experimental archaeology (focusing on pottery manufacturing and firing installations) and ethnoarchaeology (contemporary pottery craft, salt springs and salt mountains traditional exploitation). E-mail: adifex@gmail.com.

Isabella TSIGARIDA is currently finishing her doctoral research study at University of Zurich, Faculty of Arts, Department of History, on salt in the Roman Empire. E-mail: isabella@tsigarida.net.

Olivier WELLER is a research fellow at CNRS (UMR 8215, *Trajectoires,* CNRS-Pantheon-Sorbonne University, Paris, France). His research concern the archaeology of salt, specifically the origins of salt production in Europe in terms of exploitation techniques, uses and socio-economic implications during the Neolithic. The approaches he developed are both technological, ethnoarchaeological, and ethnohistorical, as well as paleoenvironmental, physical-chemical or geomatic. His study area spans from Europe (France, Spain, Germany, Poland, Romania, Bulgaria) to Oceania (New Guinea). E-mail: olivier.weller@mae.cnrs.fr.